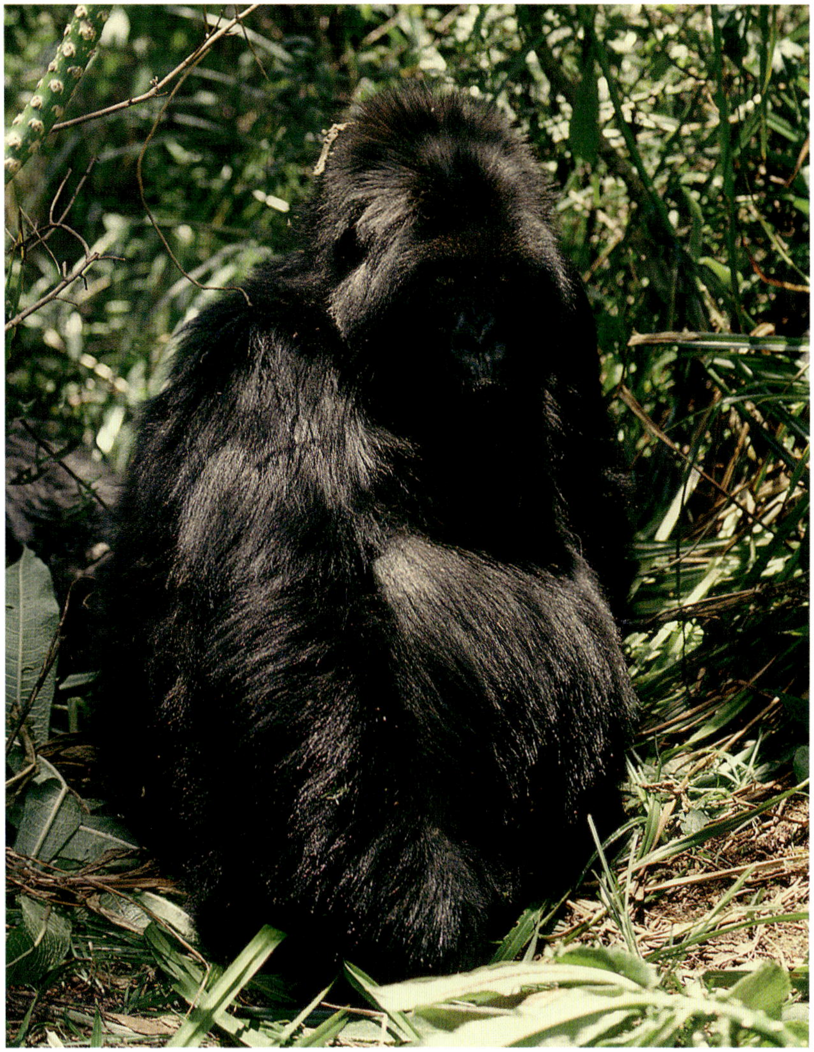

By the same author

Rabbits (A & C Black)

The Rabbit (Shire Publications)

Mice of the British Isles
(Shire Publications)

Bears (Mallard Press)

Big Cats (Mallard Press)

Secret Life of Snowdonia
(Chatto & Windus)

The Complete Owl
(Chatto & Windus)

The Great Apes (Blandford)

Wildlife of Shropshire
(Shropshire Books)

Hippopotamus (WWF/Wayland)

Grizzly Bear (WWF/Wayland)

Giraffes (WWF/Wayland)

Hidden Shallows (Quandary Press)

Wolf (WWF/Wayland)

Koala (WWF/Wayland)

Fox (Hodder)

Badger (Hodder)

Hedgehog (Hodder)

Otter (Hodder)

Deer (Hodder)

Brown Hare (Hodder)

Moose (WWF/Wayland)

Overleaf:
Mountain Gorilla
Virunga Mountains, Rwanda

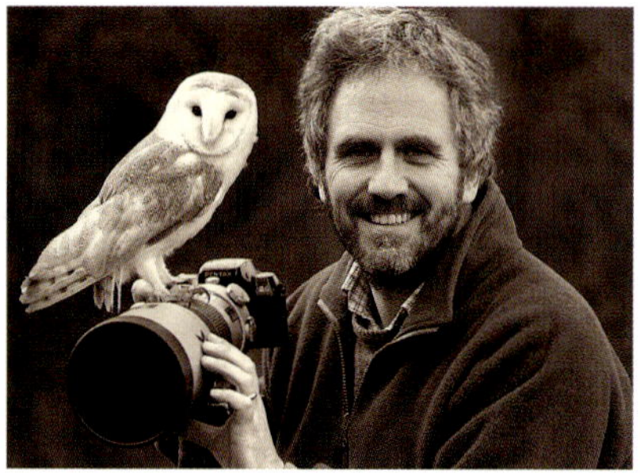

Michael Leach has been a professional wildlife photographer and author since 1977. But his career began a little uncertainly. He milked cows, sold ice-creams and worked as a petrol pump attendant before becoming established and finally making a living. Since then he has written 22 books, while his photographs have been published in countless magazines and books in over 60 countries. He has filmed wildlife programmes for both ITV and BBC.

Michael has travelled extensively in search of subjects; he has worked with many of the world's rarest and most charismatic animal species. He is in great demand on the professional lecture circuit and has been described as a 'unique wildlife humorist'. He lives in Shropshire.

The Ones That Worked

A Collection of Wildlife Photographs by Michael Leach

Quandary Press

Published by Quandary Press, Brookside, Kinnerley, Oswestry,
Shropshire SY10 8DB

ISBN 0-9540431-1-1

Designed and typeset by John Neilson, Llansilin,
Oswestry, Powys SY10 7QF

Set in Mendoza Roman and Syntax

Printed and bound by Estudios Gráficos Zure
48950 Erandio, Spain

Preface

There seem to be two popular but completely conflicting views of wildlife photography. Some people appear to think that it's simply a matter of picking up a camera and wandering around the countryside, randomly bumping into otters, badgers, owls and buzzards. If only it were that easy.

Other people imagine wildlife photographers perched on precipitous ledges, halfway up mountains for weeks on end, enduring gales and heat-stroke just to achieve that one definitive image. The truth lies, inevitably, between the two.

The vast majority of the world's wildlife photographs show the back ends of animals rapidly disappearing over the horizon, taking up five per cent of the frame. Anyone who tries taking pictures of wild animals will, at first, always produce these appalling images. Yet we show them off with pride, and enthusiastically exclaim to our friends, 'Look – there. It's a golden eagle.' Floating in the far distance, barely visible to the naked eye, there will be a vague brown blob. It could be a crisp packet caught in the breeze, or an oak leaf falling gently to the ground.

The hardest part of wildlife photography isn't taking the picture; the camera does that by itself. The real trick is getting close enough to the animal to be able to take the picture. And that is an entirely different problem. I have spent tens of thousands of hours all over the world trying to approach animals that fear the sight, sound and scent of humans. They know through instinct and bitter experience that we are the most dangerous killers on the planet. When wild animals detect the presence of a man their response is predictable, immediate and dramatic – they run in the opposite direction.

I couldn't even begin to guess the number of times I have watched as my chosen subject made a high-speed dash towards some far distant undergrowth. It is a ritual that has simply become a natural part of life. Like all wildlife photographers, a depressingly large percentage of my work ends in failure. The reasons are variable. The animals don't turn up, it rains non-stop, hordes of people appear at the wrong moment, and in Central America I was once hit by a hurricane. On another occasion a cat slept, just out of my view, directly beneath the bird's nest that I patiently waited to photograph.

My list of missed opportunities is impressive and almost endless. Fortunately, on occasions, the gods smile upon me and things go to plan. These are some of the ones that worked.

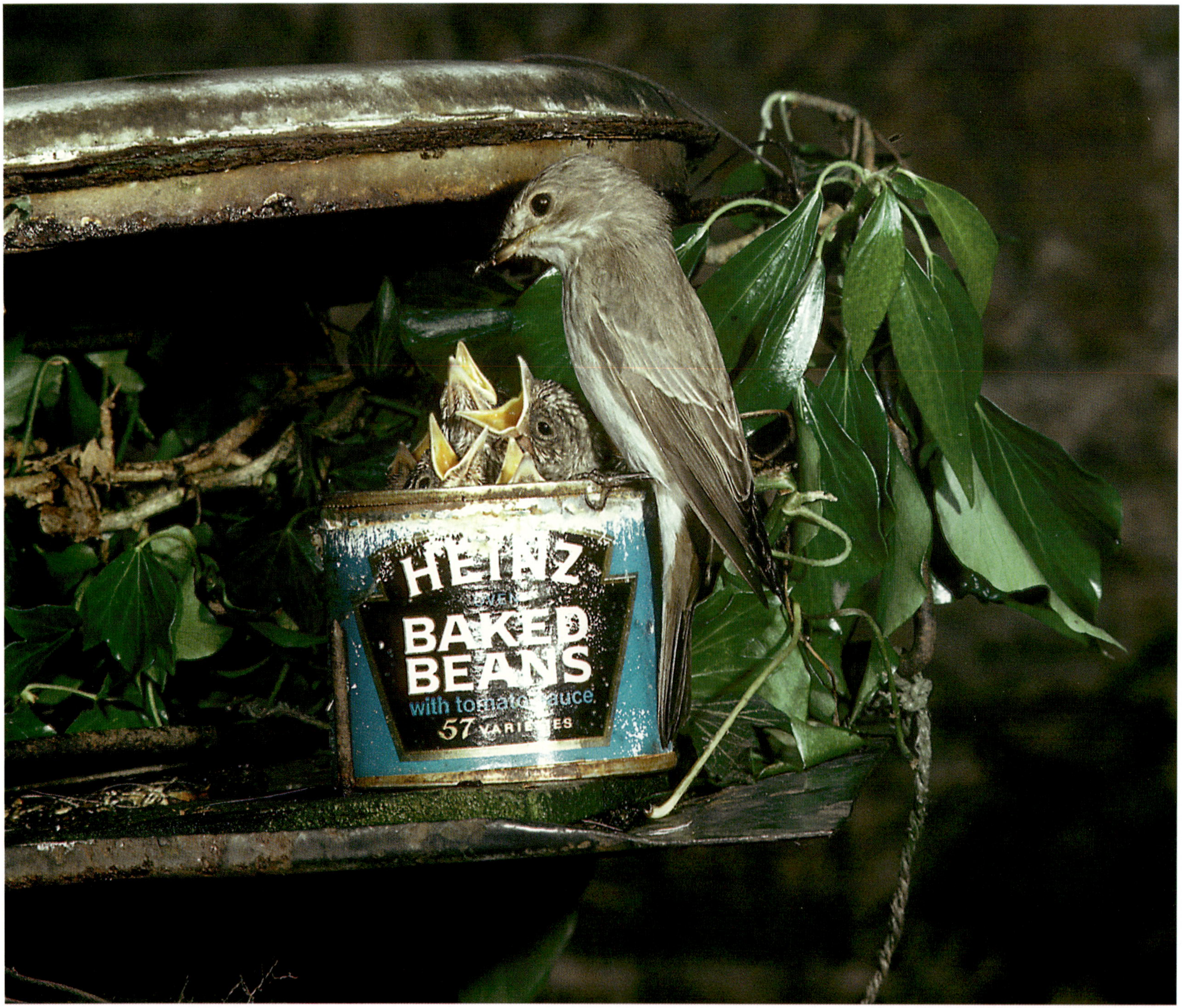
HEINZ
BAKED
BEANS
57

North Shropshire in winter can be bleak and cold. Harsh, unforgiving winds blow in from the Irish Sea and make life very difficult for local wildlife. Many birds abandon the area and fly south in search of a better climate; those that stay struggle to find food. Luckily people help by leaving out fat and peanuts, which help birds survive these hard conditions. One householder particularly enjoyed sitting inside her warm kitchen, watching birds drop onto a feeding-table outside the window. But vicious winds frequently whipped away the food and scattered it on the ground below, where the birds were hidden from her view. The lady of the house washed out some used tin cans and filled them with seeds and nuts. The wind could then do its worst but the food remained stubbornly on the table. At the end of the winter, she stopped feeding the birds but forgot to take away the tin cans.

As always the weather improved in April and the birds began to return. Amongst them were two spotted flycatchers, tiny creatures that spend their winters in Africa and return to Britain every spring to breed. Normally they search for undisturbed nest sites hidden in old buildings or behind ivy. But these two were extroverts that wanted a unique nursery. They chose an empty baked beans tin. The female spent a few days collecting moss, lichen and spiders' webs which she used to weave a soft bedding to line the cold tin. Onto this warm layer, she laid four pale blue eggs. The female flycatcher then, patiently, sat tight for the next thirteen days until the chicks emerged.

This is when the problems started because baby birds grow at an astonishing rate. Both adults ferried in a beakful of insects every few minutes from five in the morning until ten at night. The chicks were fed around four hundred times a day and grew almost visibly. In a conventional nest, made of twigs and grass, when the chicks get bigger the nest expands. Heinz baked beans tins lack this elasticity. By the time the chicks were due to leave, they were jammed in the tin like sardines. This photograph is the result of pure luck. It is simply a matter of being in the right place at the right time.

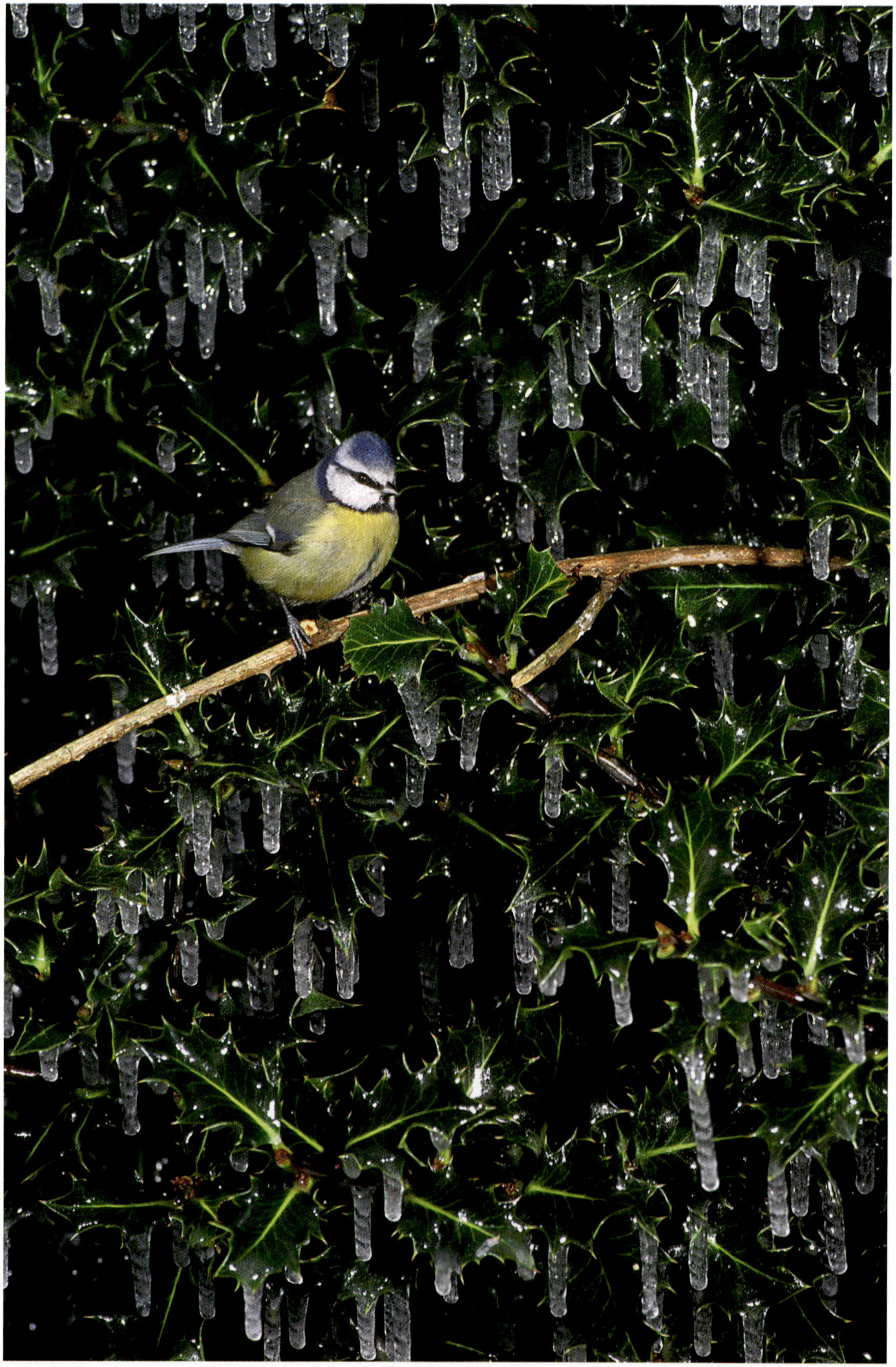

When every British bird has been photographed *ad nauseam*, it can be very difficult to come up with new ideas for pictures that will catch the eye of a viewer. A tried and trusted professional trick is to ignore the subject and concentrate on the background. I once had an idea for a winter picture that required special conditions to work; only it was two years before they occurred.

One Boxing Day evening the television weather forecast confidently stated that the country would soon be in the grip of a cold snap and temperatures would plunge down to –12°C. I gave up all idea of sleep and spent the whole night preparing for my long-awaited chance to get the picture. At 11 pm I took a bucket of cold water outside and threw it over a holly tree close to the house. Thirty minutes later, a second bucket of water was hurled over the long-suffering tree. For the rest of the night another bucket was emptied over the holly every half-hour until dawn. By 4 am the temperature had dropped to –14°C and, as the water relentlessly dripped from the spiny holly leaves, a forest of long icicles formed all over the front of the tree.

The birds in my garden had spent a vicious night sheltering from the cold, by dawn they were ravenously hungry. So I hung a bag of peanuts close to the icicles, then went inside the house to sit with a camera by an open window overlooking the holly. Ten seconds later a blue tit arrived and perched in exactly the right place. Preparation time nine hours, photography three minutes.

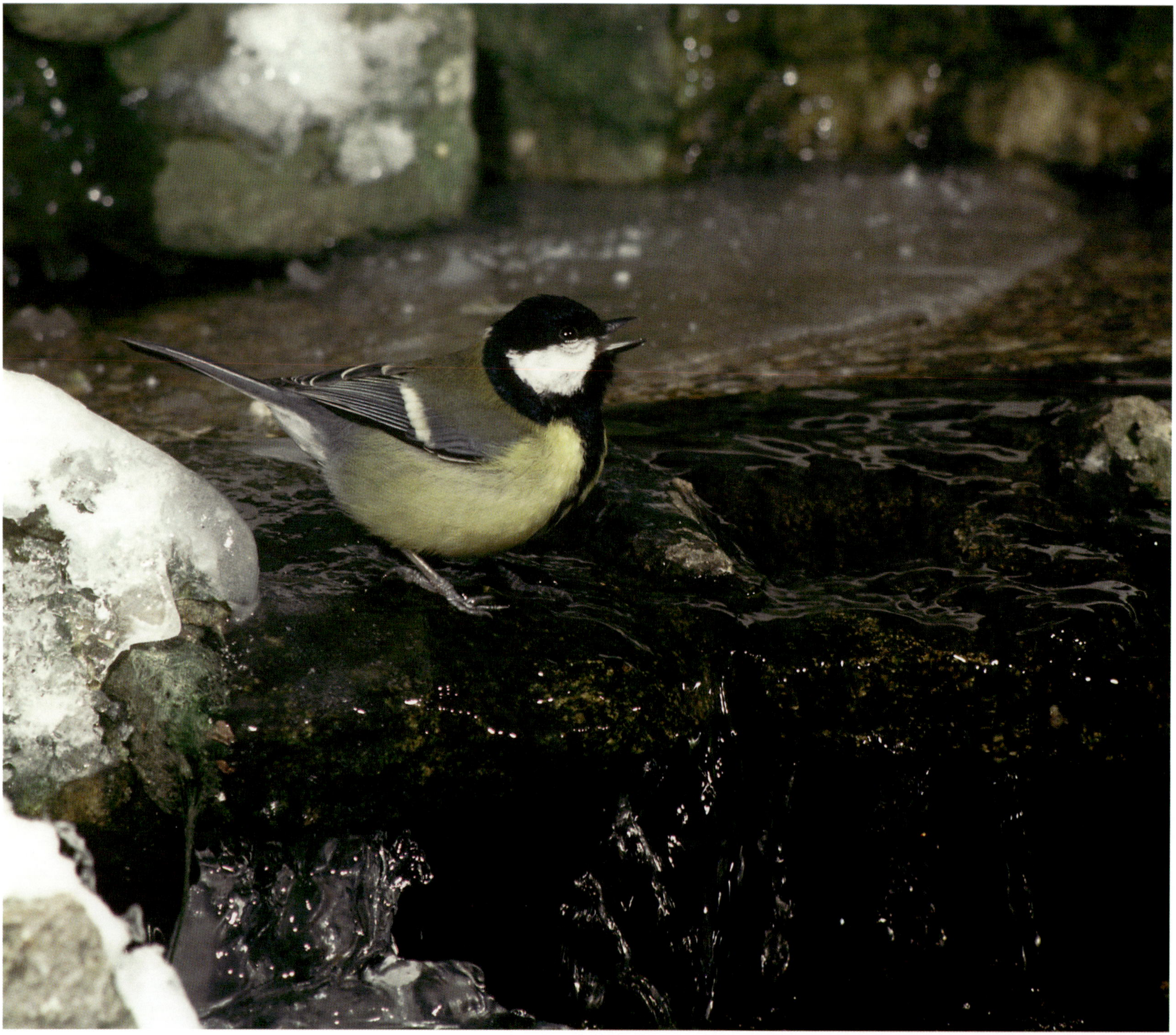

Winter is always a tricky season for wildlife photography. Days are short and cloudy, undergrowth is brown and crumpled, or completely dead. And the landscape lacks the bright colours that define the other seasons. Winter is a challenge to photographers and, more importantly, to the wild animals themselves. Food is hard to find, at exactly the time when their energy requirements are at their highest.

But lack of food is just one of their problems. Because, in the depths of a bad winter, thirst can kill just as effectively as hunger. When the temperatures plunge below zero all standing water freezes solid and it's too cold for rain. In these conditions the little available food has been freeze dried and contains very little moisture. Finding water becomes an urgent matter of survival.

Moving water freezes at a lower temperature than still water, so even a small trickle will remain ice-free while all the puddles and garden ponds around are frozen solid. Birds quickly find these oases and will travel a long way to drink. Vigils at these winter watering holes are cold and uncomfortable but the resulting photographs are well worth a little discomfort.

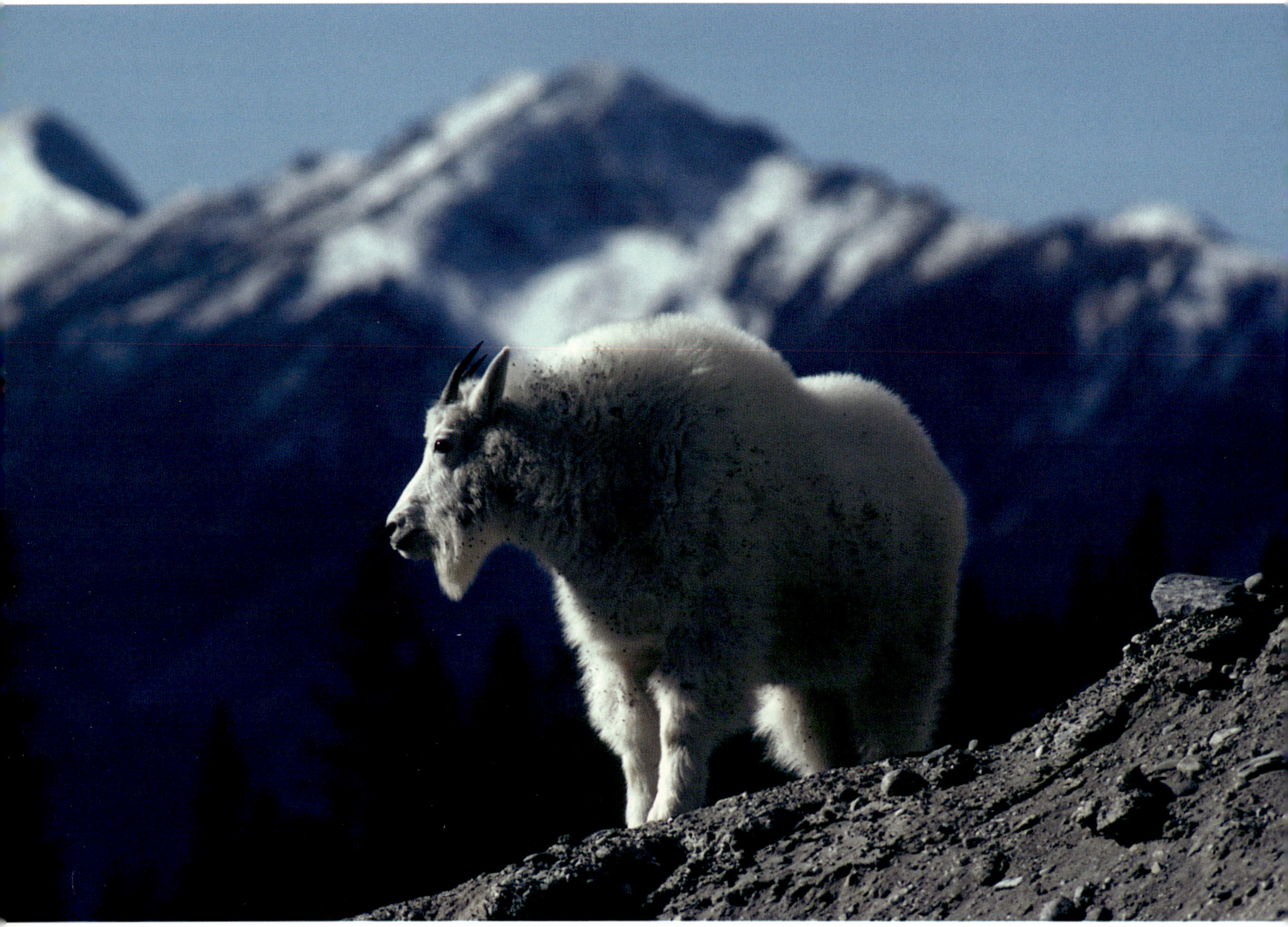

THE IMPORTANCE of finding the right background should never be underestimated. I once spent an afternoon stalking a small group of mountain goats in Yoho National Park in the Canadian Rockies. For most of that time the goats fed on an untidy scree slope that was depressingly reminiscent of a building site. I desperately wanted them to move somewhere more photogenic, but the food was plentiful so they stayed put. In the late afternoon, after a mind numbing three-hour wait the male shook himself, left the group and slowly wandered off the slope and up to a nearby summit. For a few seconds he stood in front of a neighbouring snow-topped mountain. I couldn't have chosen a more dramatic backdrop or better light. The wait had been worthwhile.

Mountain goats are strange animals that belong to a group known as the goat-antelopes. Mountain goats can only be found in the Rocky Mountains of Canada and the USA. They always live above the tree-line, feeding on moss and stunted grasses. These animals are wonderfully adapted for a life high up the steep mountains. They move with almost supernatural ease and stealth around sheer cliffs where no human could find a foothold.

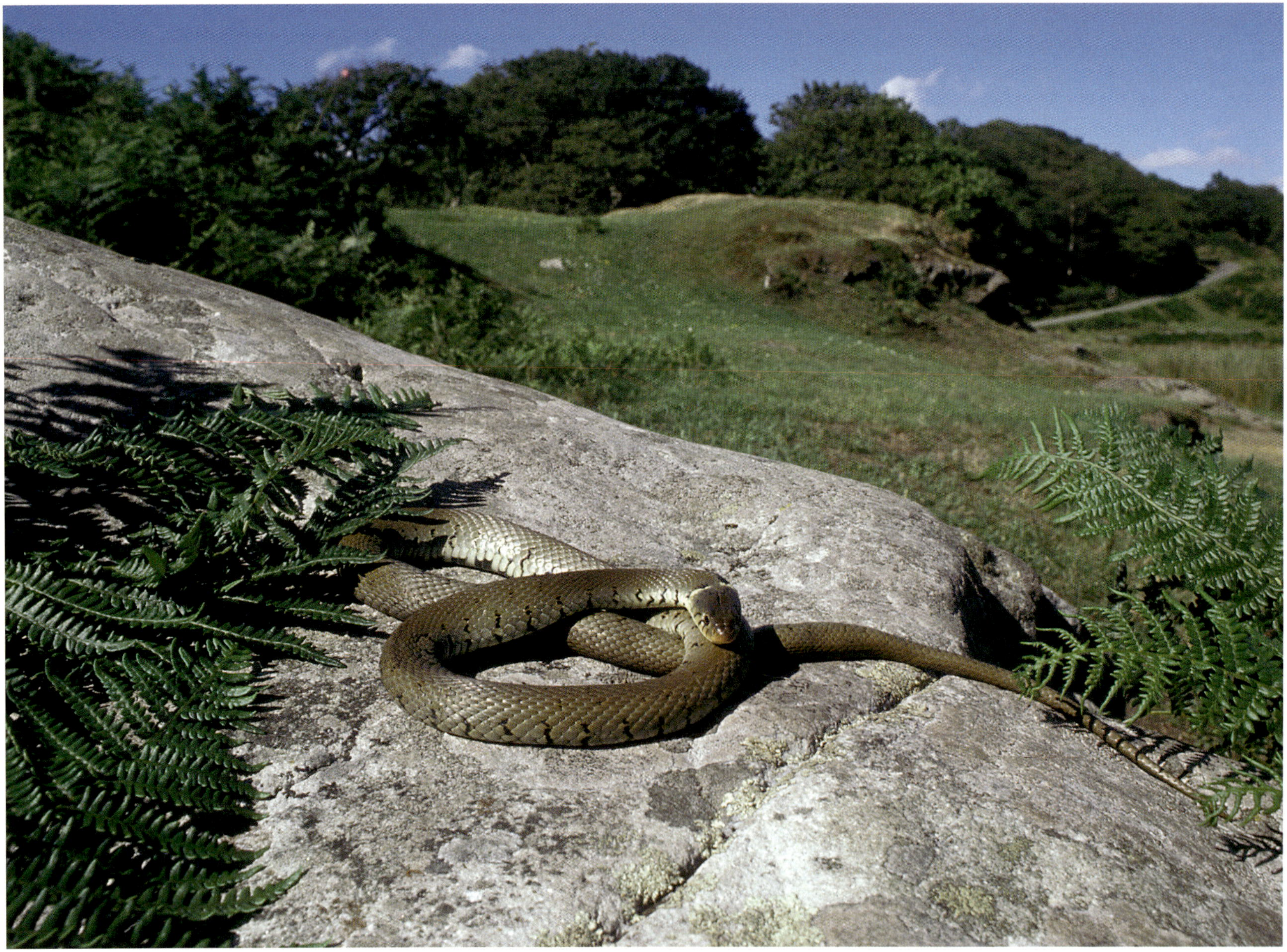

SNAKES, being reptiles, are cold-blooded. This means that they do not generate their own body temperature, as mammals do, they absorb heat from their surroundings. This cuts down their energy requirements but causes its own particular problems. In a nutshell, when snakes are cold they don't function properly; they must take in heat before they have the energy to move. After the long, cold hours of a British night, snakes, and all other reptiles, are slow and sluggish. Shortly after dawn they all try to find an exposed bank that faces the rising sun. An hour of basking allows the animals to absorb enough heat to kick-start their metabolism. Only then can they begin looking for food.

Finding snakes in the late afternoon is extremely difficult, because by that time they are usually warm, alert and fast. They can detect danger using their eyes, taste and a very keen sense of touch. If a human tries to creep close, the snake feels the vibrations of approaching footsteps and simply disappears into the undergrowth. Incidentally, snakes are deaf, as they have no ears.

The best time to photograph snakes is first thing in the morning when they are sluggish and desperate for warmth. With a little careful footwork, soft-soled shoes and plenty of luck, it's possible to creep up on a basking snake and grab a portrait that would be impossible later in the day.

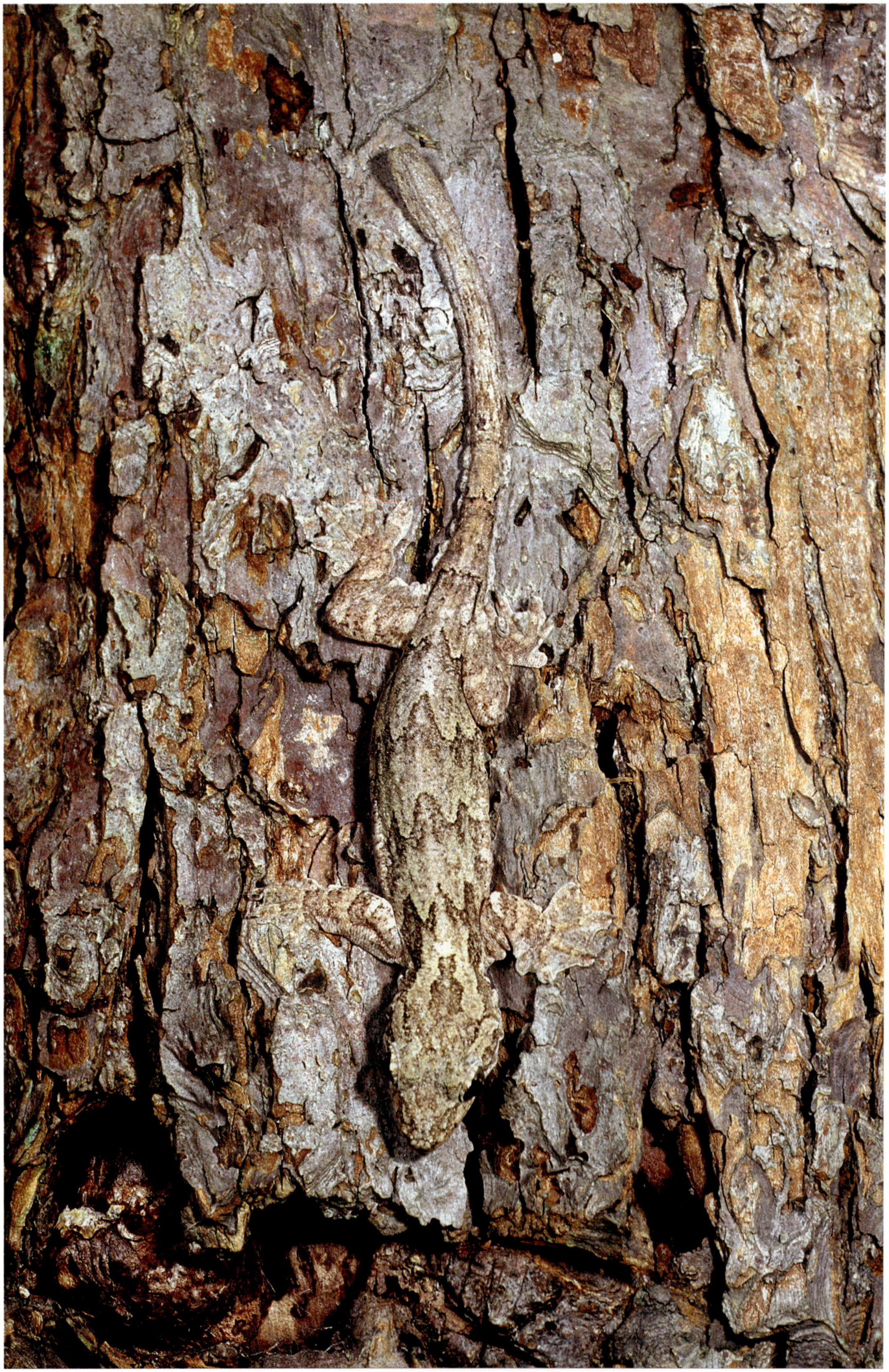

Photographing this flying gecko is no problem at all. The creature is so reliant on its cryptic camouflage, it does not even try to scuttle away.

Finding the animal, however, is a completely different matter.

Flying geckos live in the forests of south-east Asia. They spend their lives in trees, searching for small insects. But the canopy is a dangerous place: it is home to much larger animals that are quite happy to feed on any small lizard that comes their way. The flying gecko's main defence against the forest's numerous predators is an astonishing camouflage that makes it virtually invisible when it clings, motionless, to a tree trunk.
If this strategy fails, and it sometimes does, the gecko launches itself from the tree and stretches out all four legs. This action tightens a thin veil of skin tucked away on both sides of its body, between the front and back legs. Normally the membrane is invisible but when the gecko performs its dramatic star jump, the skin catches the wind and allows the gecko to .....

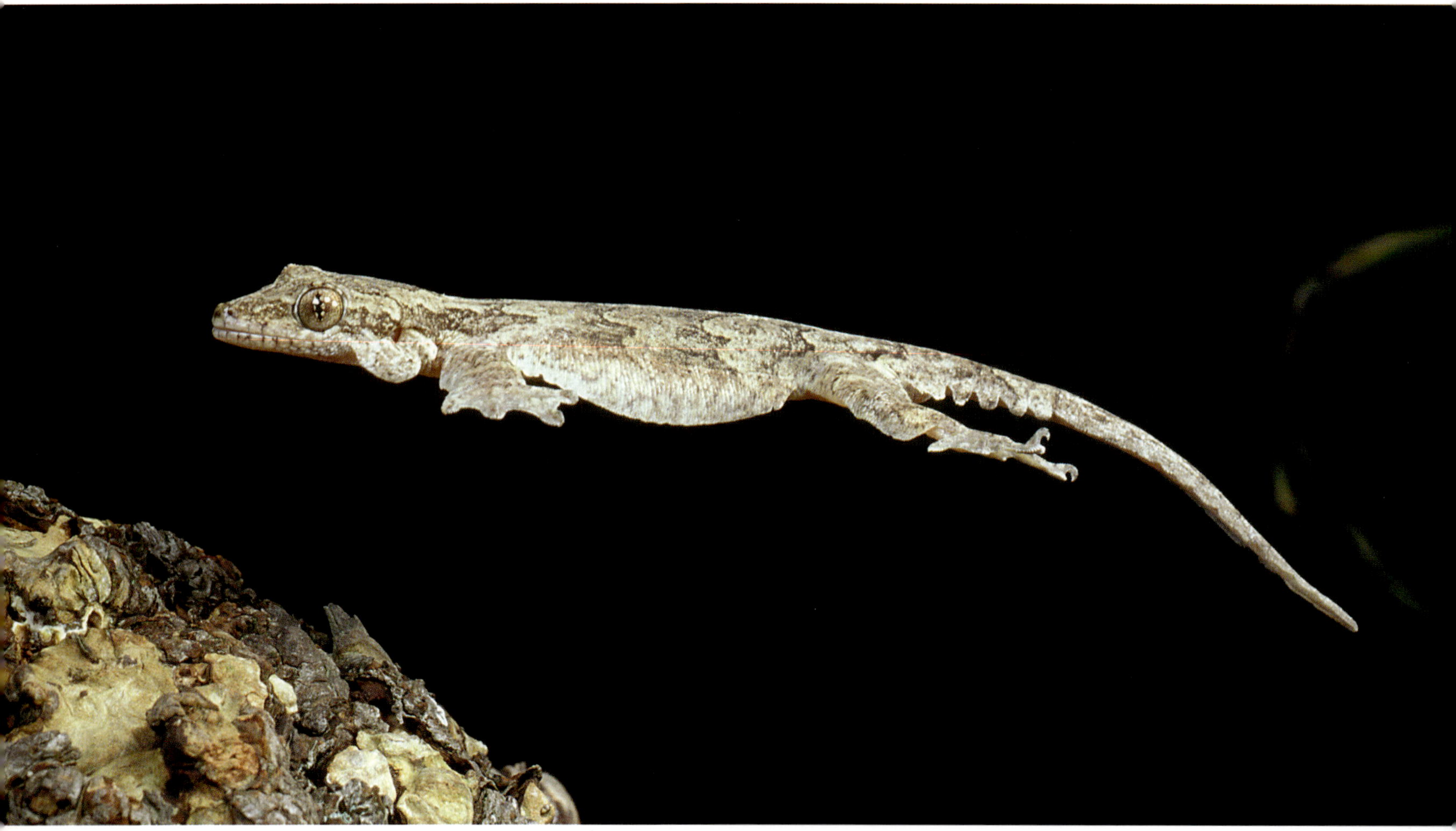

..... fly.

There are two huge difficulties involved in the photography of this kind of high-speed action. Firing the camera at exactly the right moment – and freezing the movement. These problems are both solved with some complex technology. Humans are appallingly slow when compared to the speed at which some animals move. Our reflexes are just not fast enough to follow the movement, focus the camera and press the button at precisely the right millisecond when an animal is hurtling past. So I simply let the animal take its own picture.

A beam of invisible infra-red light, just two millimetres wide, is placed across a route that is regularly used by the chosen animal. This is the trigger and is attached to a computerised control box. The camera is switched on and focused on the beam at the point where the animal is most likely to pass through. When, and if, the beam is broken, the computer fires the camera far faster than any human ever could. The animal should – theoretically – be in exactly the right spot at the right time and in focus directly in front of the camera.

Of course it rarely works out as planned. The camera will fire if the beam is broken anywhere along its path. And animals are never wholly predictable. All too often they spontaneously decide it is time to slightly deviate from the normal route, producing pictures that include simply a tail, ear, left leg or wingtip. Half the time the animal is moving away from the camera, instead of towards it. The success rate is depressingly low. And this is just one part of the system.

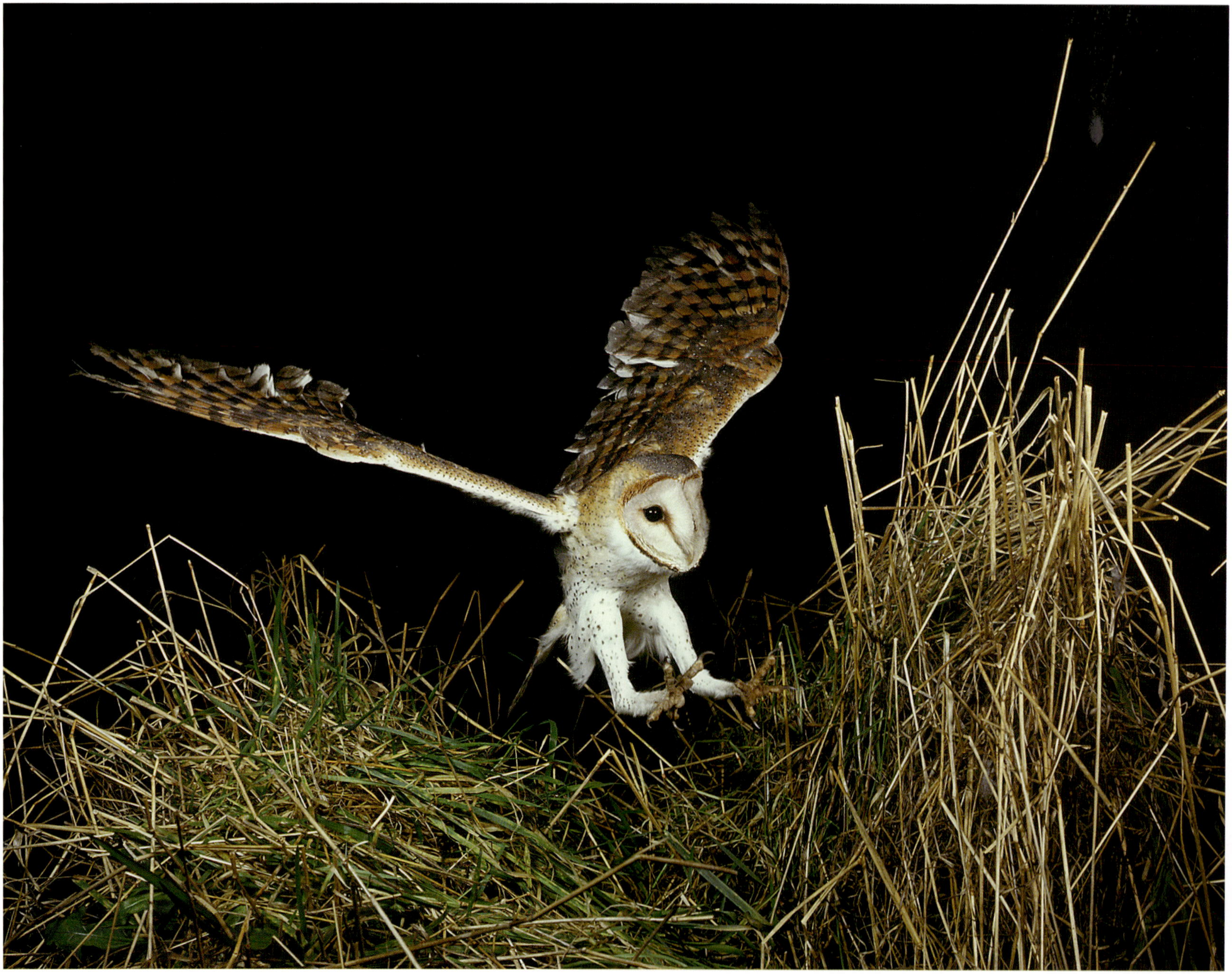

The infra-red trigger allows the photograph to be timed perfectly, but doesn't help freeze the action. That requires another set of complicated gadgetry. High-speed action is recorded on film by using extremely short exposures that observe the merest eye-blink of time. Any reasonable camera can take pictures at 1/1000th of a second, which is perfect for capturing a child on a swing or a horse jumping a fence. But it is far too slow to photograph an owl swooping at 35 miles an hour. Small animals moving at high speed simply look like out of focus blurs at 1/1000th of a second.

In technical terms, exposure is the exact length of time that light is allowed to fall onto the film. It is normally set by opening a shutter in the camera, for a fraction of a second. But there is another way. This picture was taken on an ordinary camera, using a far from ordinary electronic flash. Most flash units fire at around 1/800th of second. This system consists of three large lamps connected to a highly modified power pack; it fires at just 1/20,000th of a second. It was custom-built by an electronics expert to produce high intensity light that discharges very, very fast. The resulting flash is so short that, most of the time, it can't even be seen.

This photograph was taken in very dark conditions. When the owl flew through the beam, the computer fired the camera. And when the shutter opened, the camera triggered the flash system. Light fell on the bird for just 1/20,000th of a second. In the darkness, that was all the camera saw. That momentary twinkle became the effective exposure and, on film, the owl was permanently frozen in mid-air.

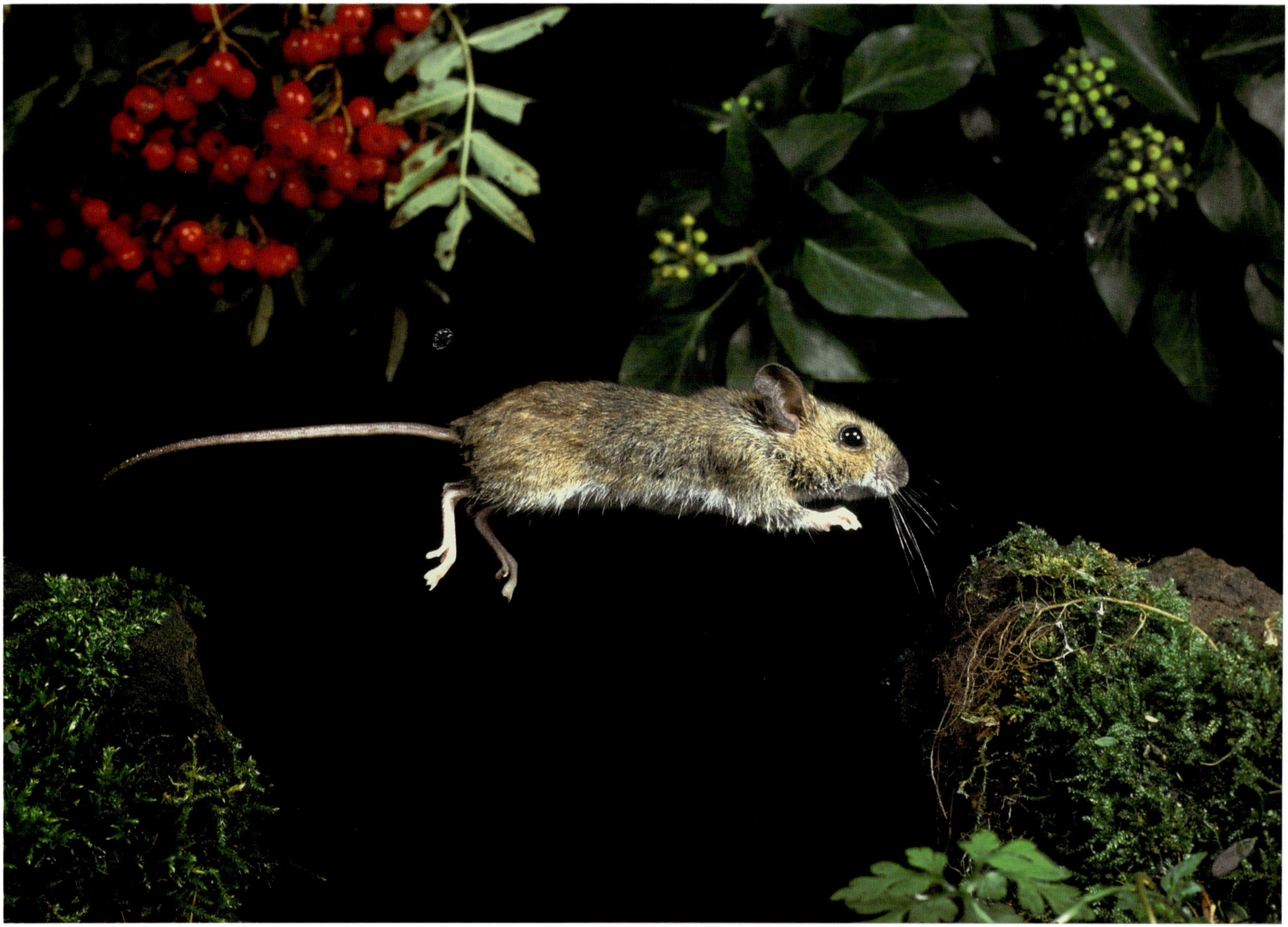

WHEN a leaping animal breaks the infra-red trigger, the movement is picked up by the control box, which instantly sends a command to the camera. The shutter opens and fires the flash guns. From start to finish this process is faster than an average human blink.

The picture of a leaping wood mouse may be simple, but the equipment certainly isn't.

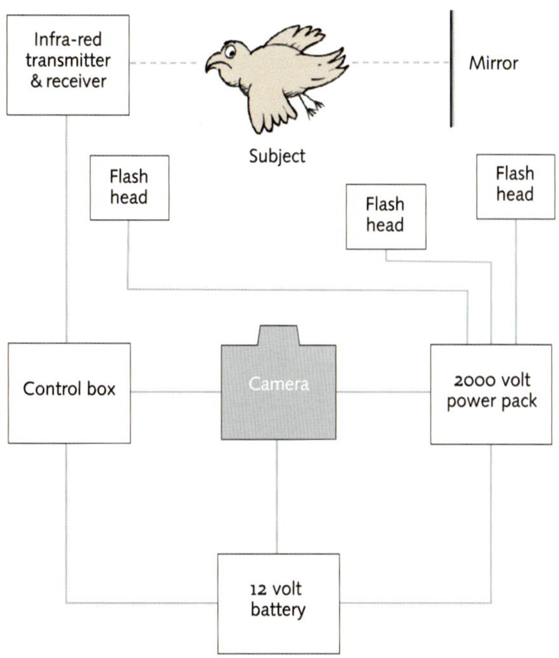

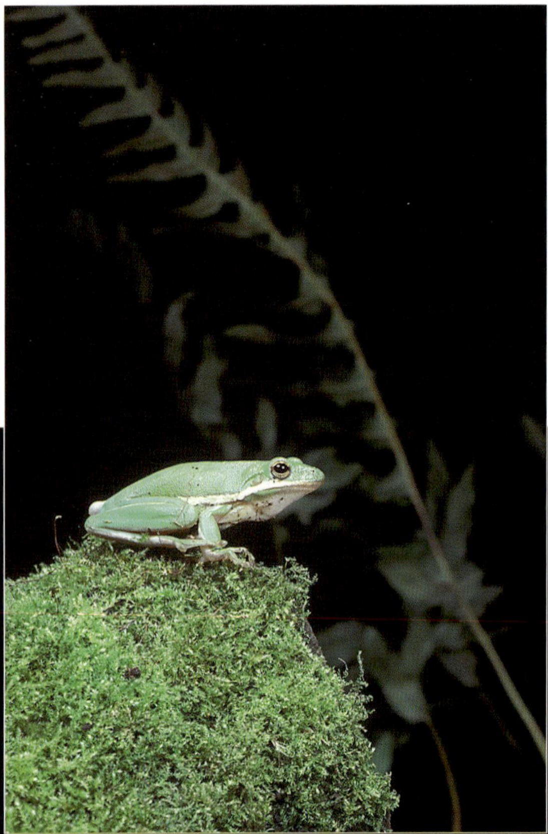

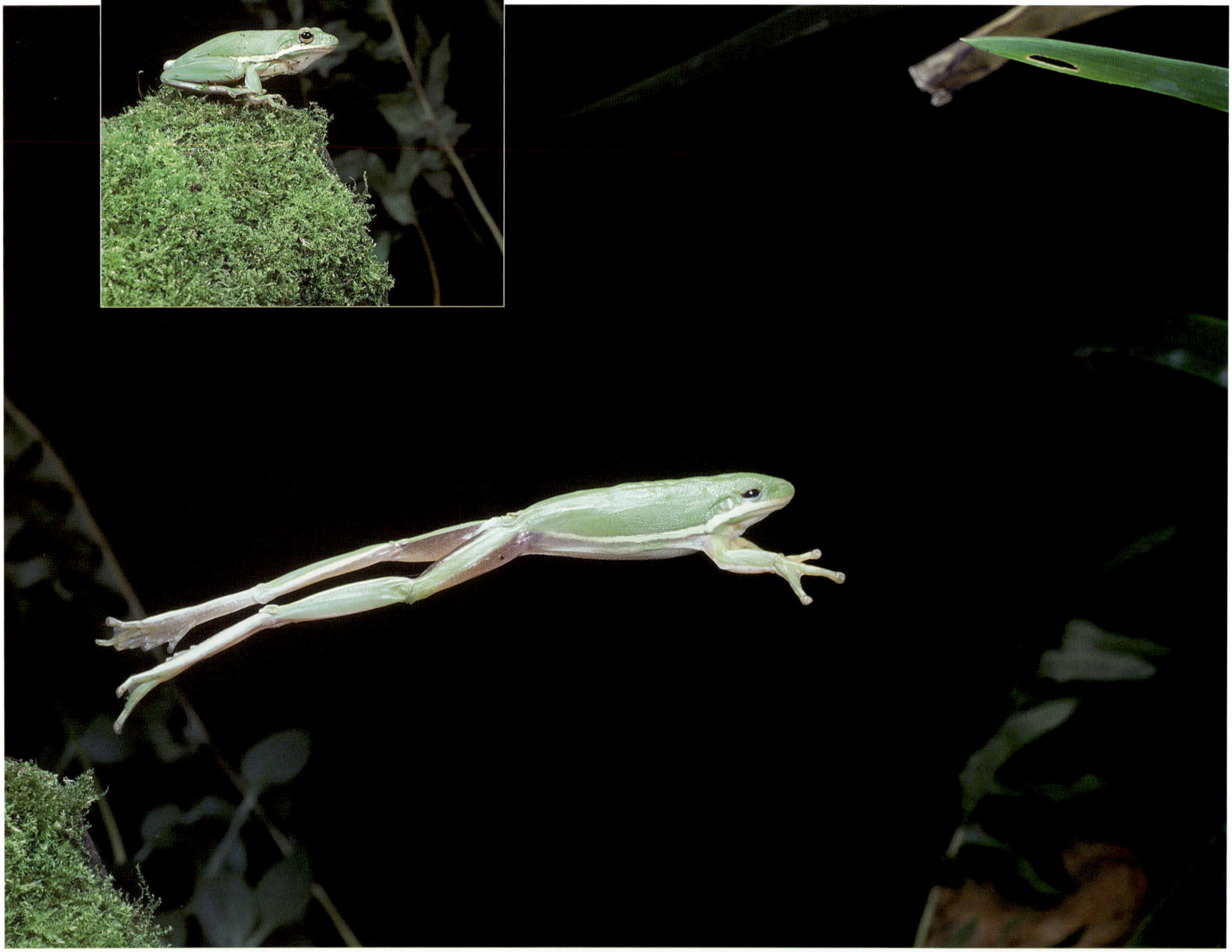

Green tree frogs are thumb-sized amphibians that live in wet, boggy areas of south-eastern USA. But they are more often seen than heard; they can be incredibly difficult to find as they hide upside down, clinging to the underside of large, shady leaves. In spring and summer, green tree frogs gather together in colonies of several hundred to perform their annual breeding ritual. The males use their strange bell-like calls to attract the attention of local females and the animal with the loudest voice wins the most mates.

Tree frogs, as the name suggests, are happy both amongst thick vegetation and in the water. They have specially adapted toes that are fitted with tiny tread-like pads that help them cling to even the smoothest surface. The toes also produce mucus which has a very strong surface tension that helps the frog stick to almost anything. Tree frogs are accomplished, if slow, climbers that are permanently vulnerable to attack by larger animals. When danger threatens these tiny amphibians leap wildly in any direction, covering a distance that is out of all proportion to their size. It is a highly successful survival mechanism.

Sitting motionless, the tree frog hardly produces a dramatic portrait but at 1/20,000th of a second a tree frog in mid-air shows the true beauty of these wonderful and unexpected creatures.

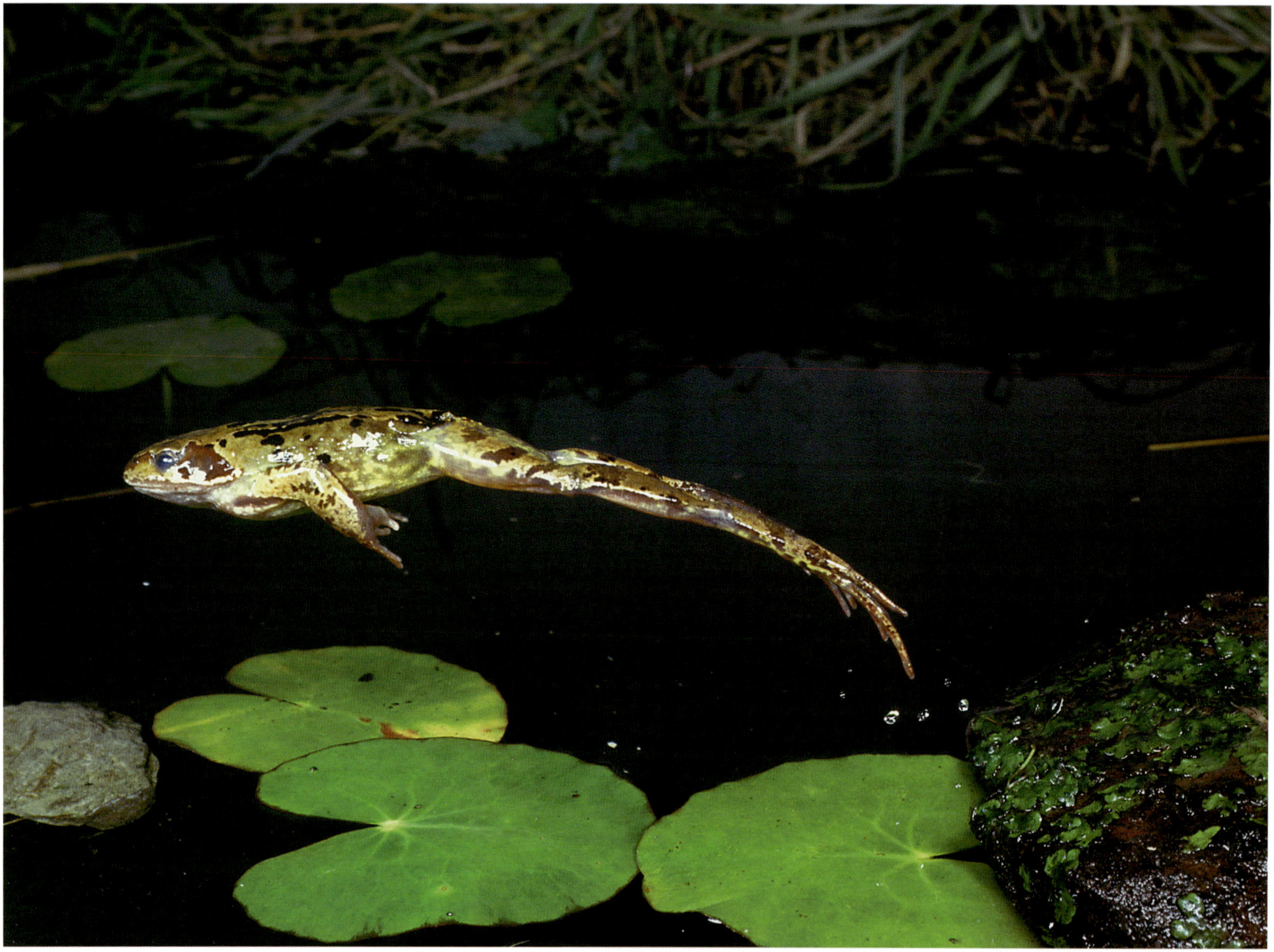

Even the humble British frog can look elegant and athletic when caught in mid-leap across a garden pond.

But all is not as it seems. The high-speed equipment is costly and replacing it would be hideously expensive. Like most electrical gadgets the infra-red trigger and flash system is sensitive to water. It would be sheer lunacy to balance this temperamental technology over a muddy pool in the vain hope that a frog might jump through.

So a much safer pond was built in my studio. It was made in a shallow wooden box, with a plastic liner, and then filled with a mixture of rainwater and mud. Visible areas of plastic lining were covered with chunks of turf and after standing for a few days the water looked convincingly pool-like. Two genuine rocks were taken from my real pond outside and carefully positioned as frog take-off points. A few water-lily leaves scattered on the water surface completed the effect.

The equipment was switched on and the trigger was aimed at the edge of the rock. I then went out to examine the resident frog population in search of a prize specimen. This particular frog was an easy winner. The others were muddy brown, mustard yellow or black. This one has a wonderful bronze glow. I put the frog on the rock; he immediately jumped off, took his own photograph and was carried back to his real home.

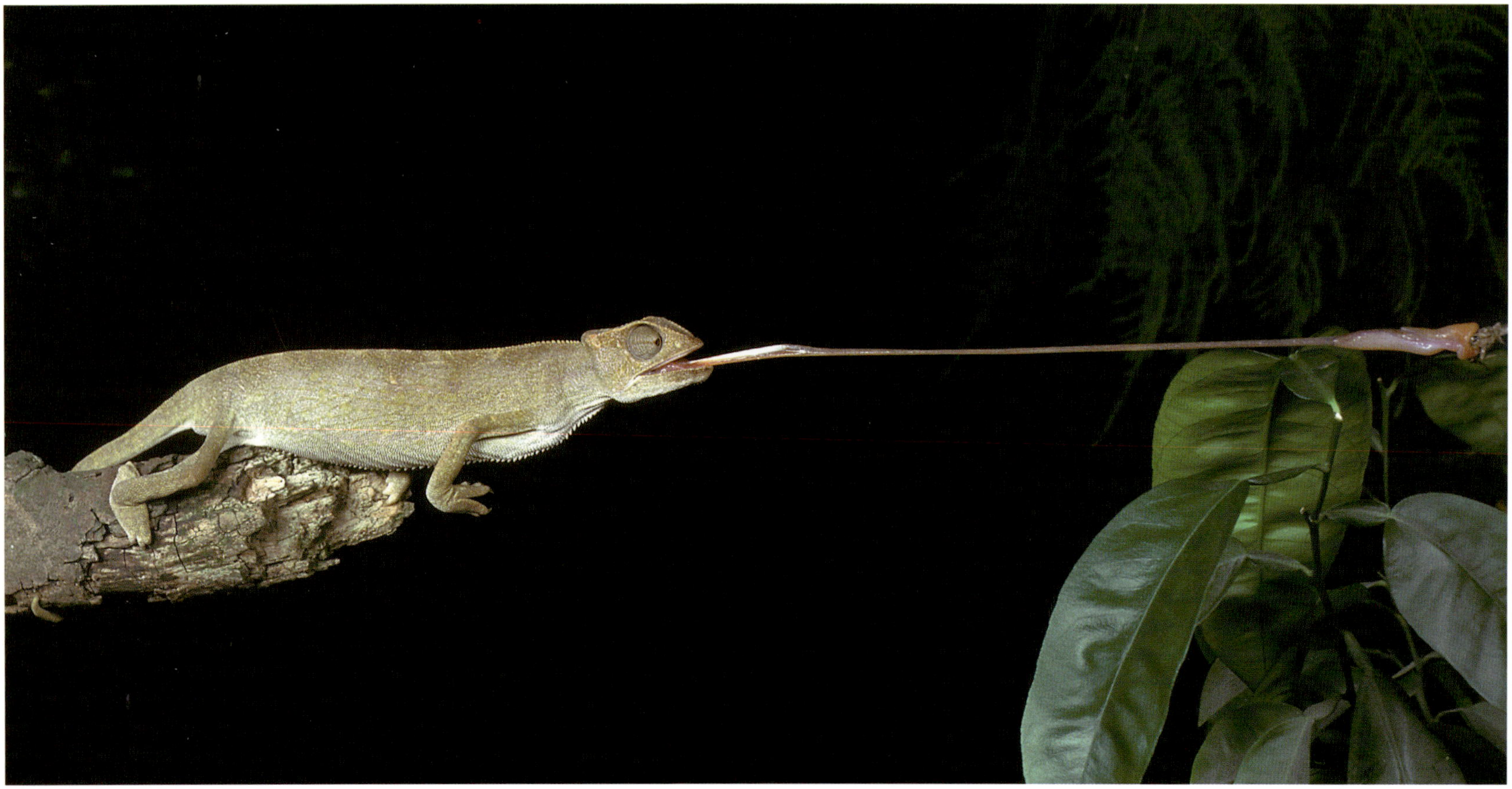

Chameleons are rightly famous for their extraordinary ability to change colour but they have other, less celebrated skills.

Chameleons are slow-moving creatures that never come out of second gear. They only eat insects, but don't seem to have the physical equipment to catch food that can disappear faster than the eye can follow. To compensate for their lack of speed, these reptiles have evolved a tongue that, at first glance, looks completely impossible. A chameleon's tongue is almost as long as its body – it doesn't need to pounce or sprint. A hunting chameleon moves arthritically slowly; sometimes it's impossible to tell that they are actually going anywhere at all. An unsuspecting insect would not be even vaguely troubled by the appearance of such a sluggish, clumsy creature that was sitting on a branch too far away to be a threat. It is a fatal error. Half a second later the insect has vanished and the chameleon is still in the same place. In a movement too fast to follow, the chameleon's tongue snakes out across the void. With unerring accuracy the tongue hits the prey and captures it with a sticky pad on the very tip. The kill is made and nothing seems to have happened – unless we can freeze the action in mid-flow.

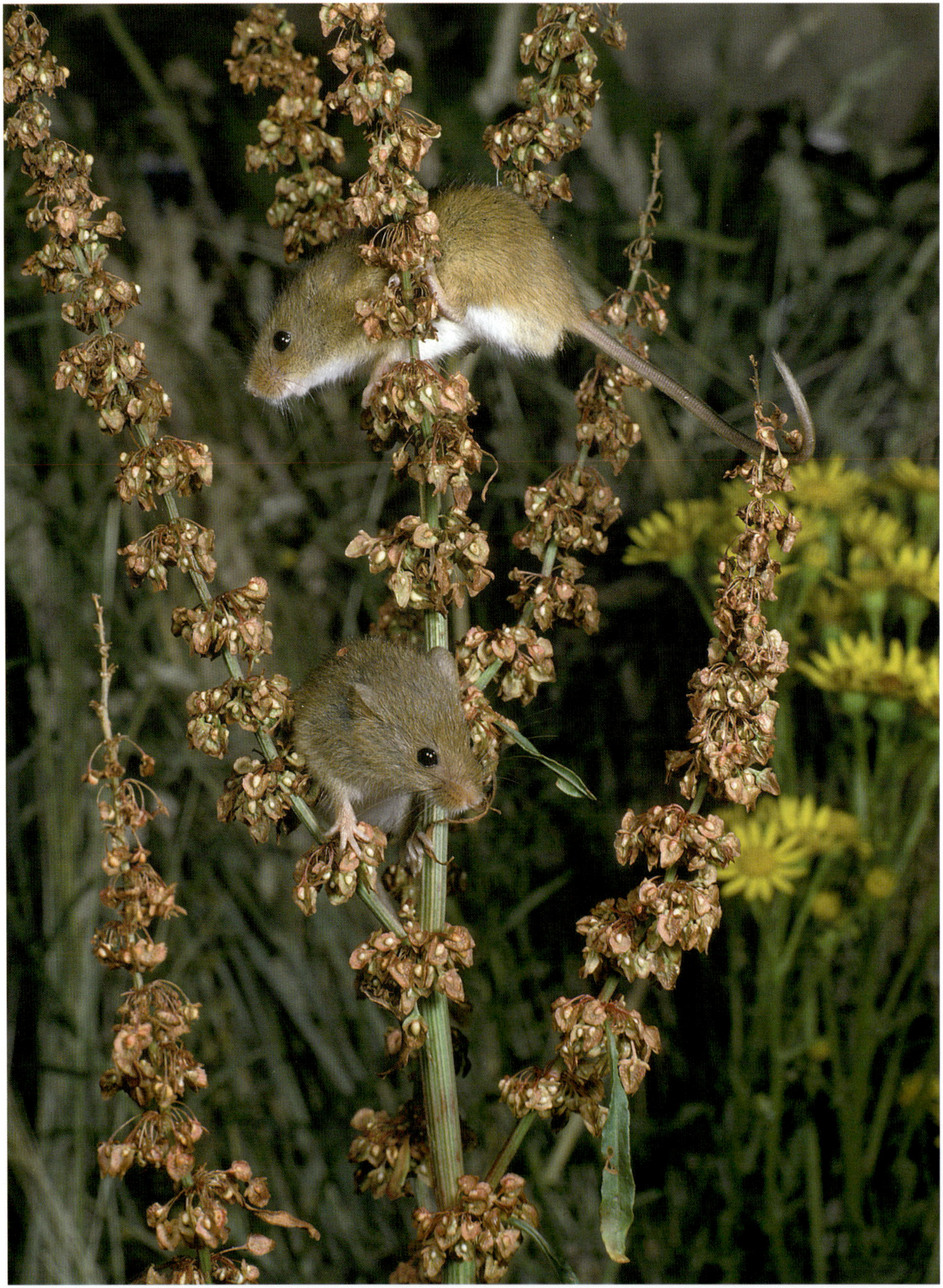

As a basic rule of thumb large mammals are easier to photograph than small ones. There are exceptions, but this is a good starting point. Big animals have fewer enemies and can often defend themselves when necessary. Small creatures face a far bigger army of predators; fear and suspicion are their main form of defence.

Small mammals have evolved an impressive battery of early warning alarms that alert them to the presence of such dangers. Acute hearing and eyesight, together with a sense of smell that we can only imagine, provides a 360° enemy detection system that makes photography virtually impossible. So wildlife photographers need to be ..... creative.

If the animals cannot be photographed in the wild, then we simply bring them into a studio and make them *look* wild.

The real skill of this technique is to build an environment that is utterly convincing. And that is much more difficult than it sounds. Leaves must face the right direction, grass must look fresh and green rather than recently mown; the combination of plants must be exactly as it would be in a natural setting. It has to look just like the corner of a field or the centre of a bush. Part of the skill is to choose precisely the right background for each species. As their name suggests, harvest mice are normally associated with fields of crops such as corn and wheat. This was accurate two centuries ago but modern technology has changed the mouse's landscape. Gentle fields of golden-headed crops are not the peaceful islands of tranquillity they appear. A gang of men would once have taken several days to cut and strip a large field. Today the same area is collected, sorted and baled in just a few hours by a single man in an air-conditioned harvester. These fields have become death traps for small animals that are not fast enough to escape the relentless machines.

Harvest mice survived long before humans introduced intensive agriculture, so they have simply adapted their behaviour yet again. The greatest numbers of these charming animals are now found on quiet roadside verges and in thick hedges. For this picture I simply fitted out a glass tank to look like an overgrown and neglected corner of a meadow.

The choice of studio sets completely dictates the atmosphere of the photograph. These are harvest mice and this, of course, is.....

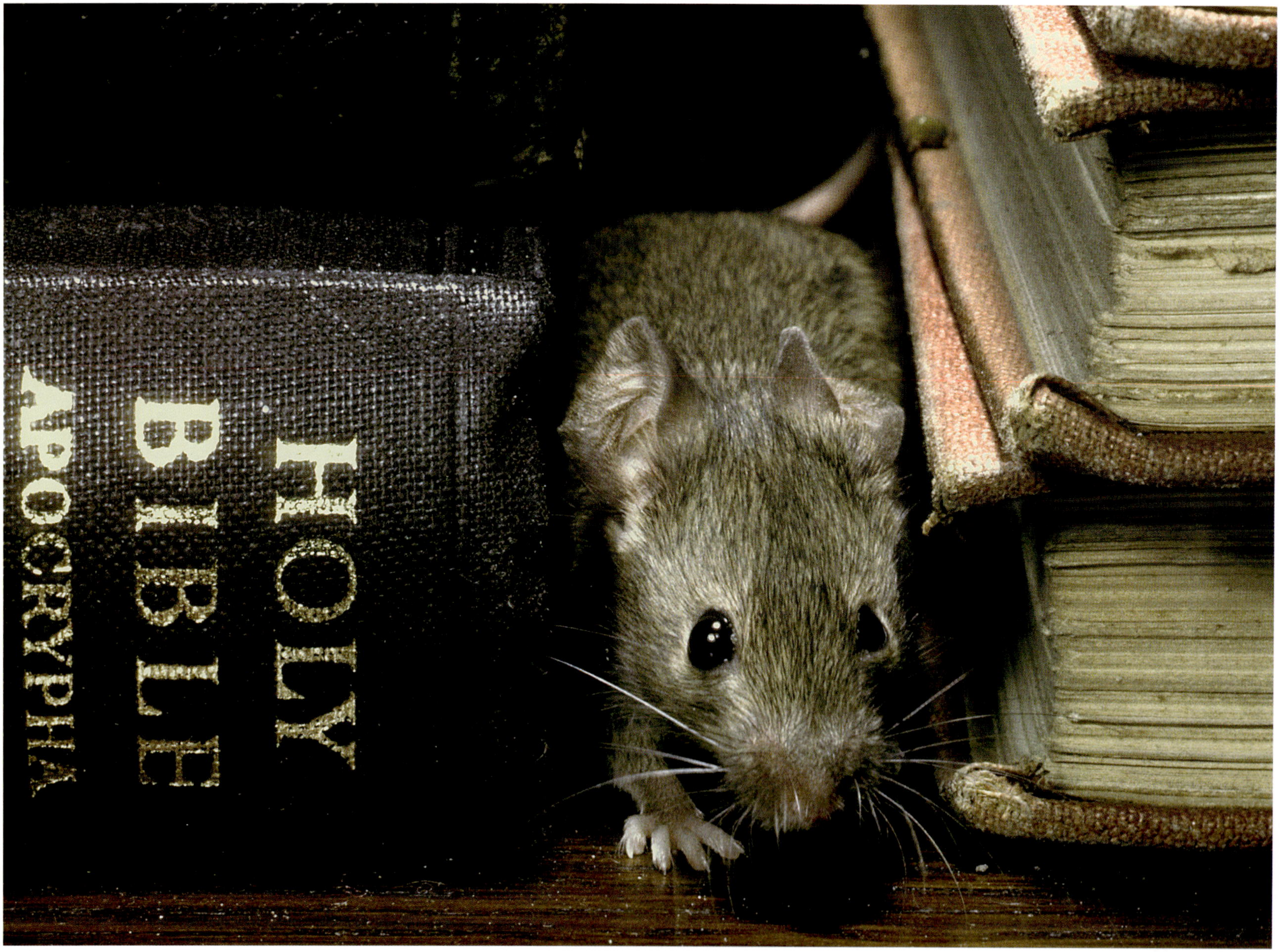
HOLY
BIBLE
APOCRYPHA

.....a church mouse.

There are, believe it or not, stringent ethics applied to this blatant manipulation of reality. We never use wild mammals for photography. In a studio they would behave exactly as they would in the outside world. One sniff of a human and any well-balanced mouse would panic and dive for cover into the carefully constructed undergrowth. It would be a traumatic experience for the animal and photography would be impossible. Studio sets only work when the animals are completely at ease. So we use individuals that have been hand-reared in captivity. The stars of my mice pictures came from a friend carrying out research into rodent behaviour. They were all as daft as a brush, quite happy to sit on my hand and feed. Amongst their carefully constructed background they can explore and feed in safety, totally untroubled by either the human or his camera.

This picture is made, without any doubt, by the choice of book on the left-hand side. If the spine had read 'The Merchant of Venice' or 'Pride and Prejudice' it simply wouldn't have worked at all. Each time this photograph has been reproduced in a book – and it has happened often – the caption writer uses the inevitable 'church mouse' reference. This was no accident.

The animal, by the way, is a house mouse. And for the record they don't much like churches. There's not enough to eat.

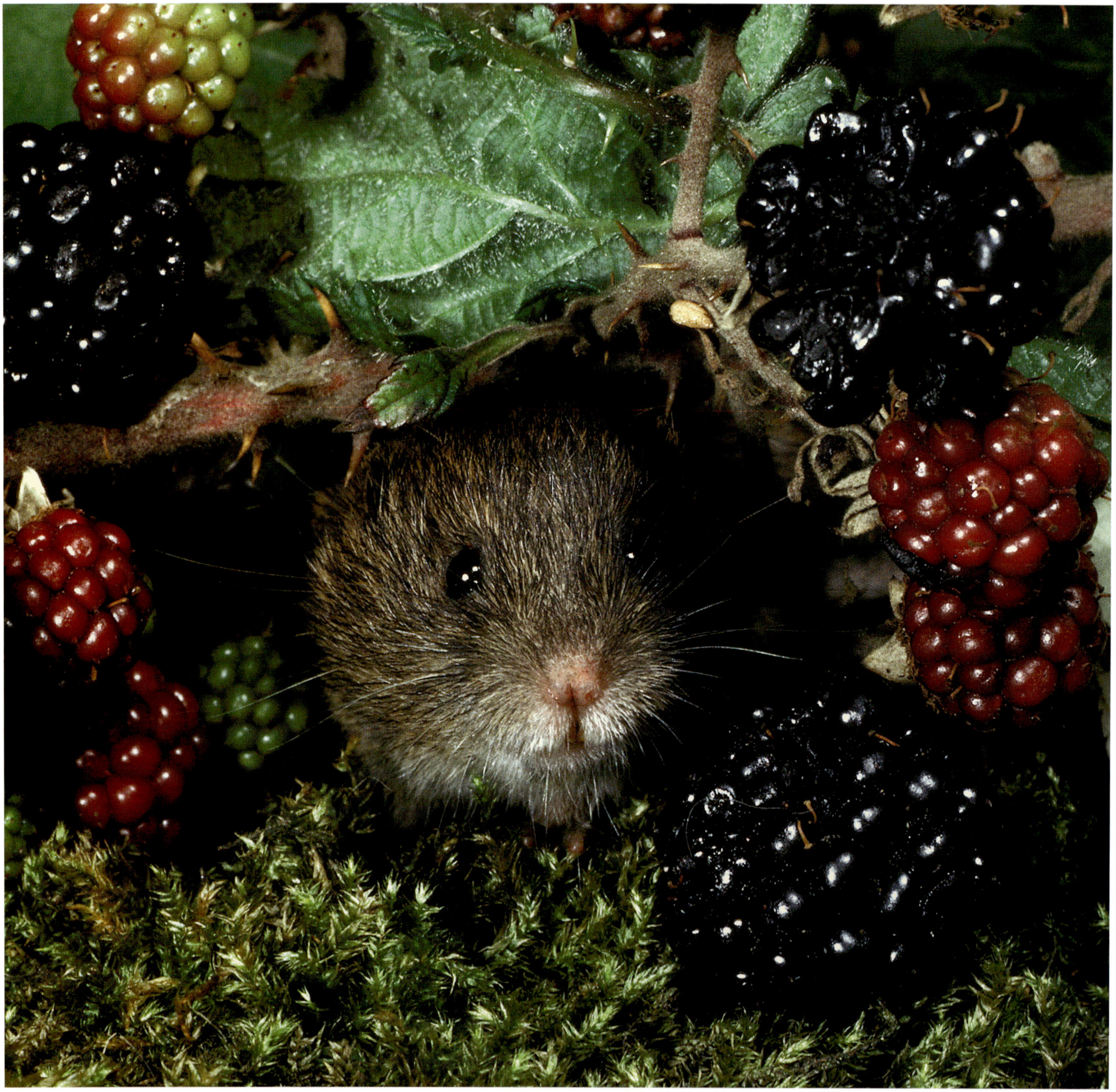

Autumn is probably the best season for wildlife photography. Natural colours are at their most spectacular and the choice of available 'props' is almost infinite. Fruit and nuts are particularly effective additions to any background, for very basic reasons.

One American psychologist believes that all humans are subconsciously drawn to images that contain edible subjects. The vole in this photograph plays only a supporting role. The ripe, glistening, luscious blackberries are far more appealing than the small furry head of a rodent that few people could identify. The species of animal is irrelevant, the spot where it appears is the heart of the photograph.

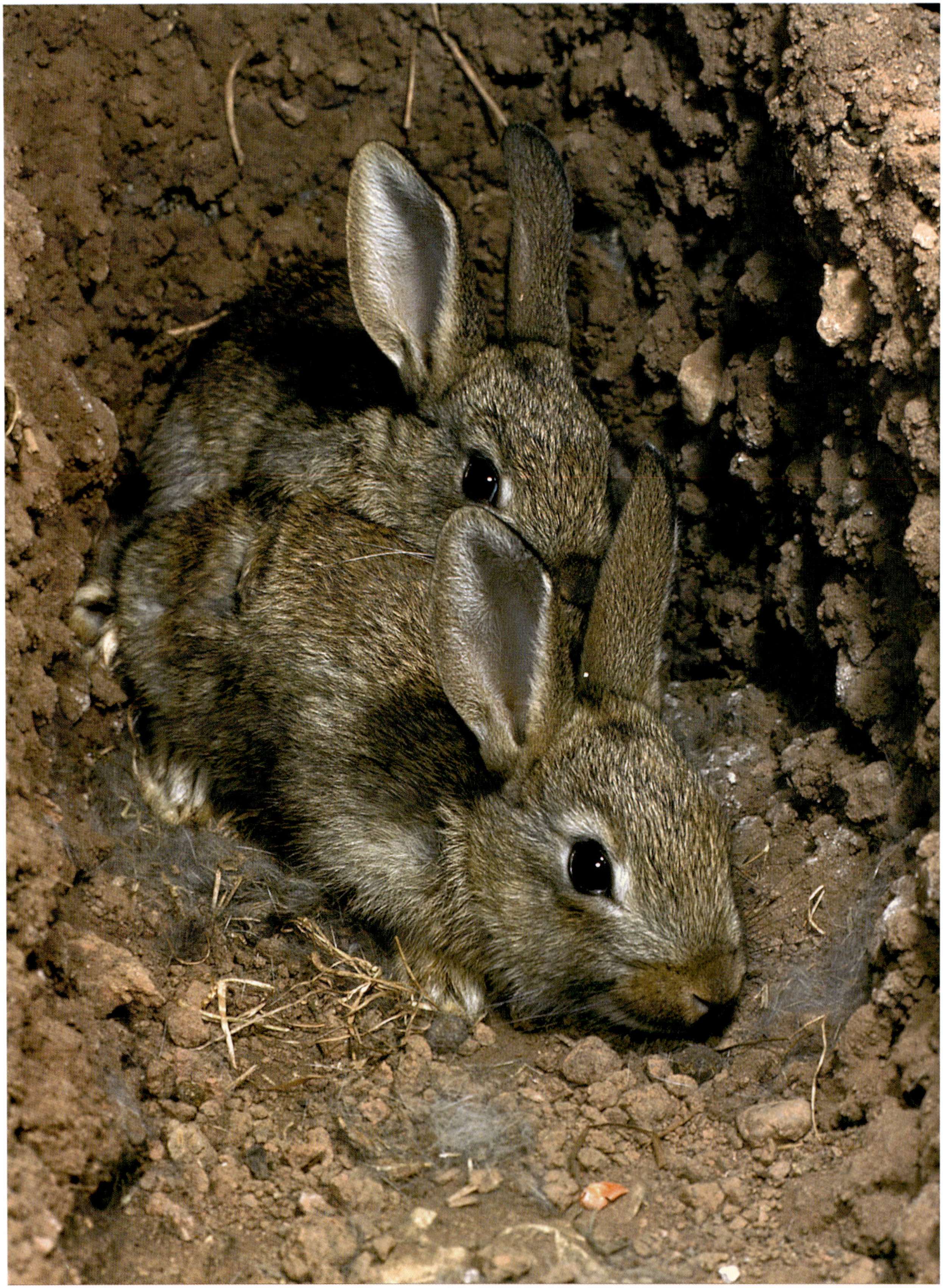

Although most studio sets are simple, others need to be much more complex and time consuming if they are to work. I always find it surprising how rarely people consciously analyse wildlife programmes and photographs. We live in a cynical age and have learned to question almost everything around us, yet mysteriously wildlife has avoided the probing gaze of the general public. Sometimes it is worth giving a few seconds' thought to the process that produced these evocative images that fill our books and screens.

Take, for example, a shot of a rabbit giving birth in an underground den. Do you really think that the pregnant doe sits waiting patiently in her tunnel while the cameraman spends hours with a shovel? Speaking as a professional it would be delightful if the female rabbit obligingly produced her offspring when the camera and lights were in place. But it simply isn't possible. Wild rabbits bear no resemblance to their cute and cuddly popular image; they are tough, suspicious, highly efficient survivors. A pregnant doe's immediate reaction to any form of disturbance is to reabsorb her unborn young back into her own body system. She just wouldn't give birth if there were any kind of outside interference. These pictures have to be taken under controlled conditions by recreating a rabbit warren in a studio. It's a tried and trusted technique that you have, unknowingly, seen many times before.

Step 1 Build a wooden box and create the basic shape of the tunnel with lengths of wood.
Step 2 Cover the wooden skeleton with strong wire mesh.
Step 3 Cover the wire with papier-mâché and wait until dry.
Step 4 Coat papier-mâché with a thick layer of glue.
Step 5 Add soil. This must be *thrown* on, not tapped down with hands as this leaves tell-tale fingerprints.
Step 6 Wait until dry and add tame rabbit.

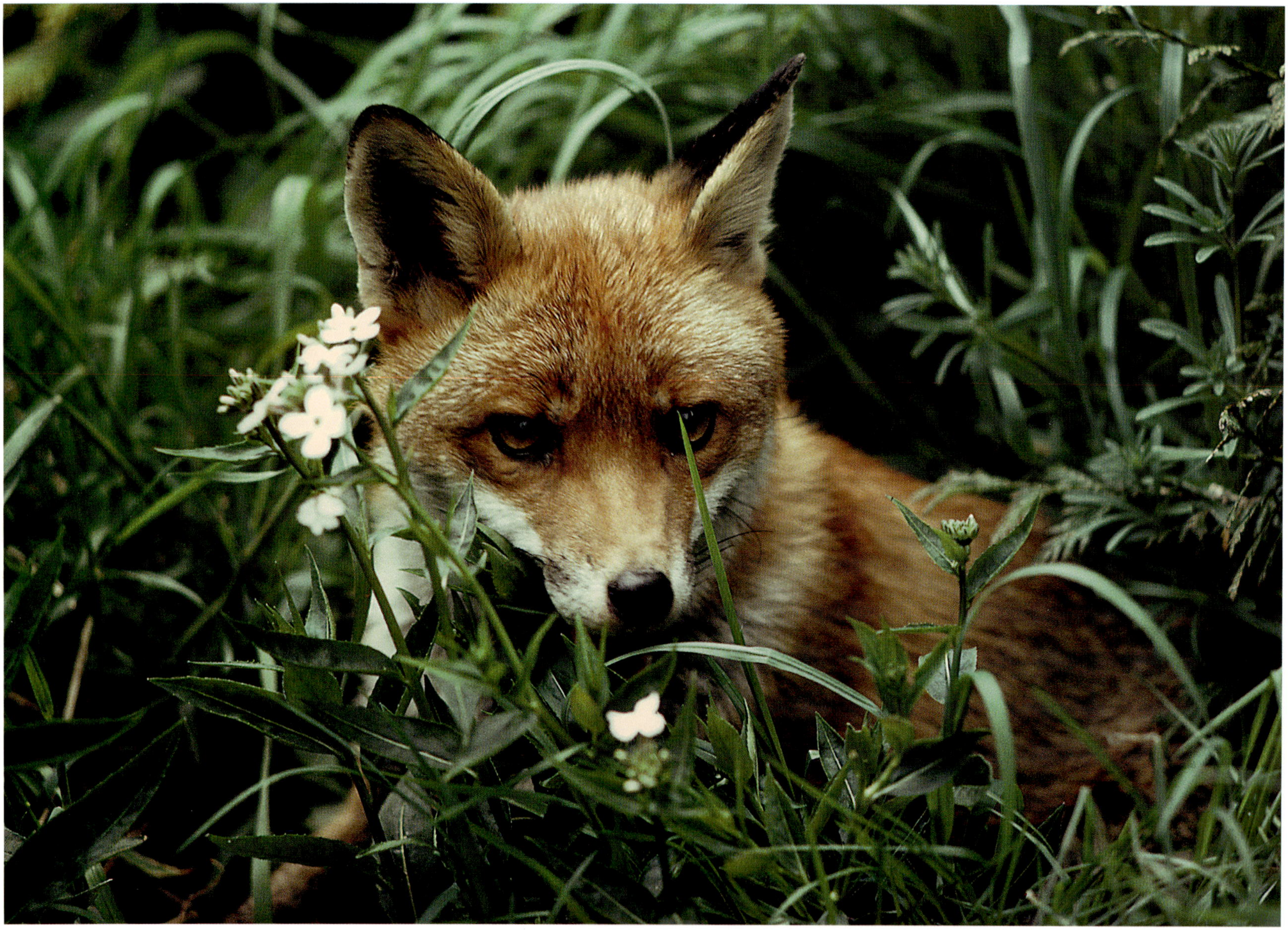

A LOT OF WORK has been done on how people analyse photographs. We understand precisely what is appealing and what is distressing. We also know exactly what you look at when seeing a picture for the first time.

If the image is a portrait, of either a human or animal, the very first thing you will notice are the subject's eyes. Direct eye contact is a basic communication strategy for all primates, including humans. We can, unknowingly, gather a wealth of subliminal information by looking at the eyes of a friend, rival or enemy. All of us, automatically, look at eyes – and this knowledge is very useful to photographers as it can cover up all kinds of technical shortfalls.

When taking a picture of any animal, it is vitally important to focus on the eyes. If they are alert and sharp the whole picture will work. If the eyes are dull or out of focus, the entire image will be ruined. I have to admit that this is not a perfect portrait, but it has still been hugely successful and has appeared in dozens of publications. But the ears are not quite sharp and the tip of the nose is slightly out – only none of that matters because you are looking at the fox's eyes.

Always focus on the eyes whenever taking a photograph of any animal. It's one of the completely unbreakable rules.

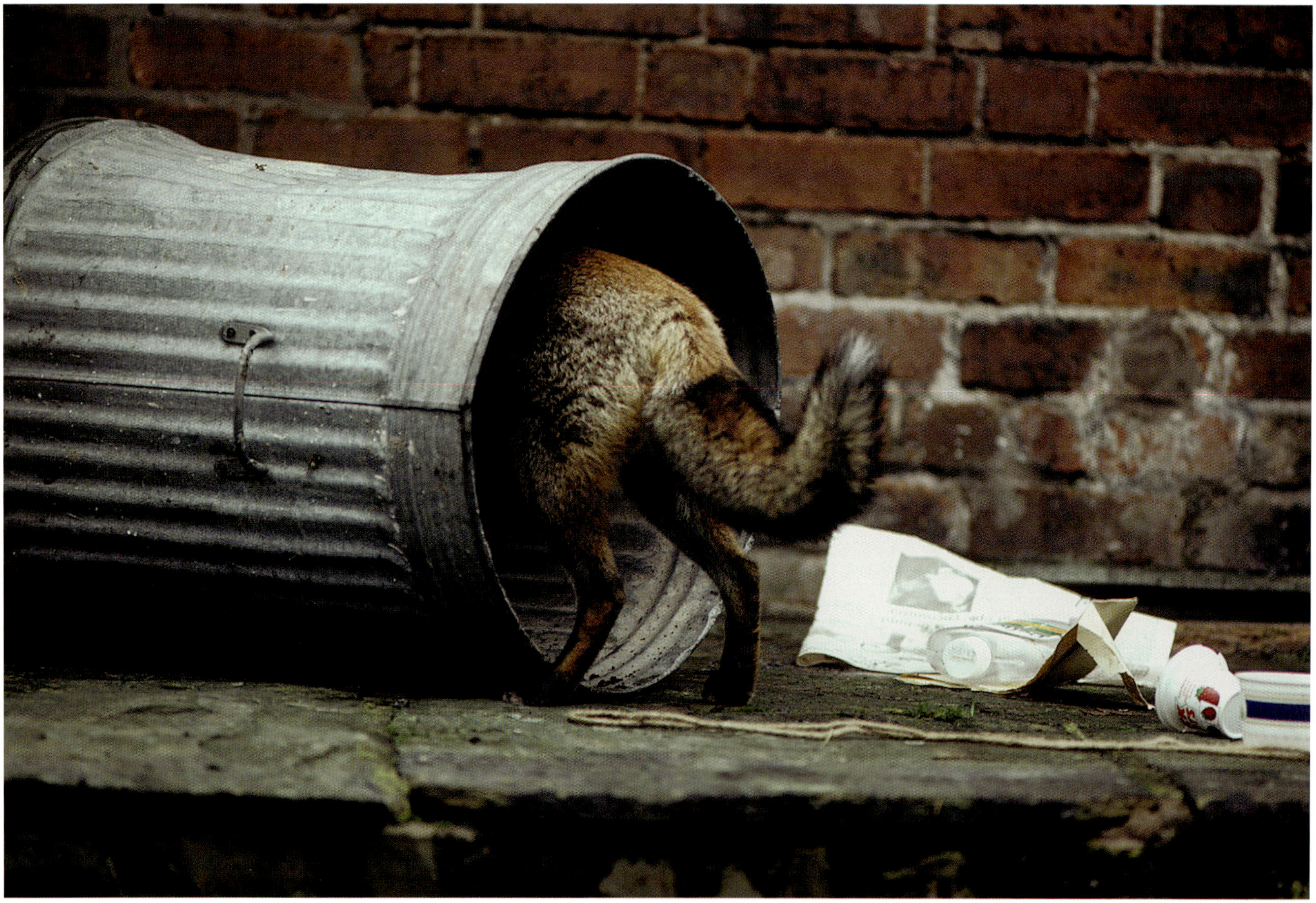

Of course, as with all completely unbreakable rules, there are plenty of exceptions.

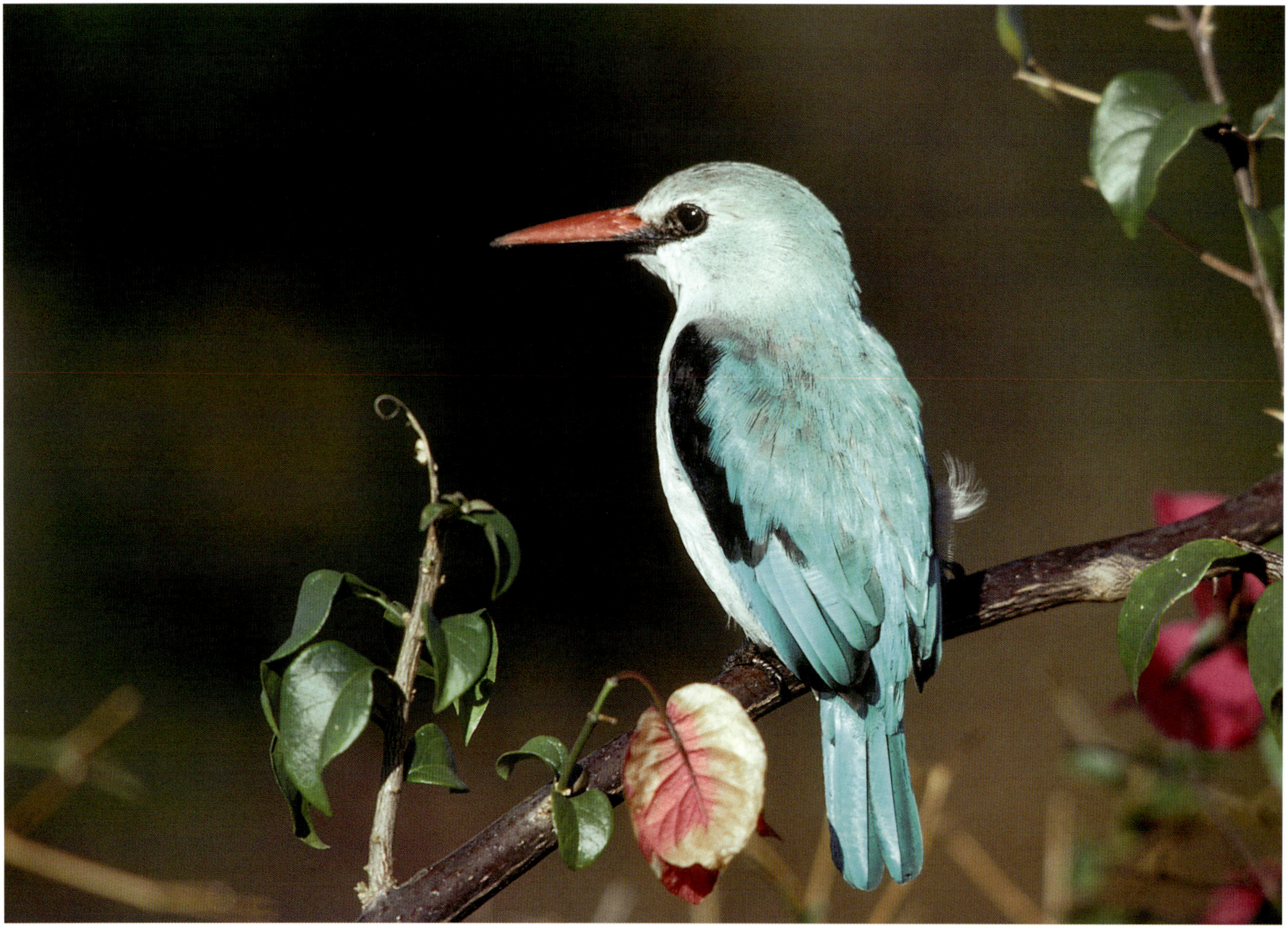

I ONCE SPENT a long, hot, dusty day driving through the Masai Mara in Kenya in search of black rhino. Not long ago these huge animals were found over much of Africa but they are now depressingly rare, as I found to my cost. After twelve hours of searching, there was no sign at all of the elusive rhinoceros and the low sun showed it was time to go back to camp for a shower. As I unloaded the cameras from the jeep, there was a sudden blur of turquoise in the trees in front. A woodland kingfisher landed on a thin twig and sat in the last rays of evening sunlight.

The kingfisher stayed for more than a minute, which is an eternity in terms of wildlife photography. Using the camera that had been waiting, fruitlessly, all day to capture a rhino, I grabbed my best ever pictures of one of Africa's most beautiful birds. In less than sixty seconds I ran off a whole roll of film of the kingfisher in perfect lighting, sitting in a spot that was impossible to beat. Wildlife photography is often a matter of luck. Of both kinds. It's usually not possible to record bad luck, as the subject simply never turns up. But sometimes the tables turn and along comes an animal that I would never normally have attempted to photograph this way.

Despite their name these kingfishers don't eat a lot of fish. They feed mainly on insects, along with the occasional lizard. Which is why I found the bird hunting in dry forest well away from any water.

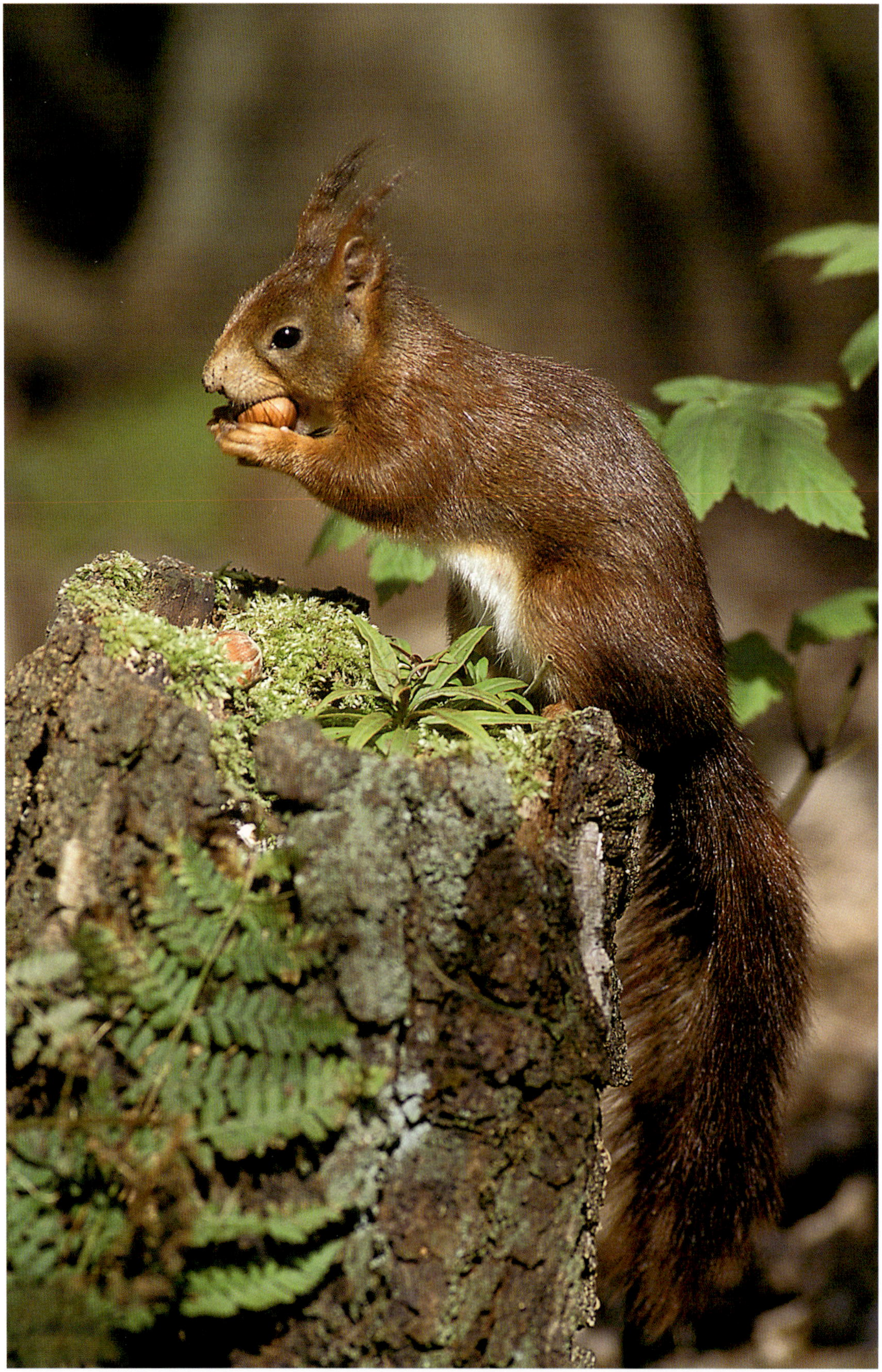

Research is the most important part of wildlife photography, particularly when working with unfamiliar animals. It's absolutely essential to know where they can be found, what they eat, what time they appear and all the other nuggets of information that will allow us to get close.

Before ever picking up a camera I read books, search the internet and ask experts. Somewhere amongst that tangle of detail there are always clues that lead to the right time, place and approach.

Red squirrels are a perfect example of why research is so important. They are a common species in some parts of Scotland and the Lake District. But they are also nervous and wary of humans. It might be tempting to pick up a telephoto lens and drag it around the conifer plantations of the Highlands, but all you will see are trees. On a very lucky day you might just catch a fleeting glimpse of a rust-red tail disappearing into the tree tops. Small mammals are frightened of us. We arrive and they disappear: it's a basic law of wildlife. Luckily this law is not universal; a spot of in-depth digging will usually unearth some unlikely place where things are done slightly differently. There is at least one nature reserve where red squirrels have learned to accept humans, because visitors pay their dues in the form of nuts.

The resident squirrels have grown up knowing that they can approach humans and expect food. But they have become increasingly sophisticated with time. Most visitors simply arrive with a packet of unshelled peanuts. Some red squirrels would regard this as manna, but these gourmets have higher expectations. Over the years they have become very particular feeders. Anyone offering a mere peanut will be greeted with an annoyed flick of the tail and then treated to the sight of a rapidly retreating squirrel. Aspiring squirrel watchers need to go armed with the ultimate food – hazelnuts.

The formula is absurdly straightforward. Spend some time discovering where to find tame squirrels. Look around for a photogenic background that would look good on a picture. Offer a hazelnut to the best looking squirrel available – just to catch his interest. Carefully lead the squirrel to the chosen spot, using the nuts of course. Hide a pile of hazelnuts where they can't be seen by the camera. Take some photographs.

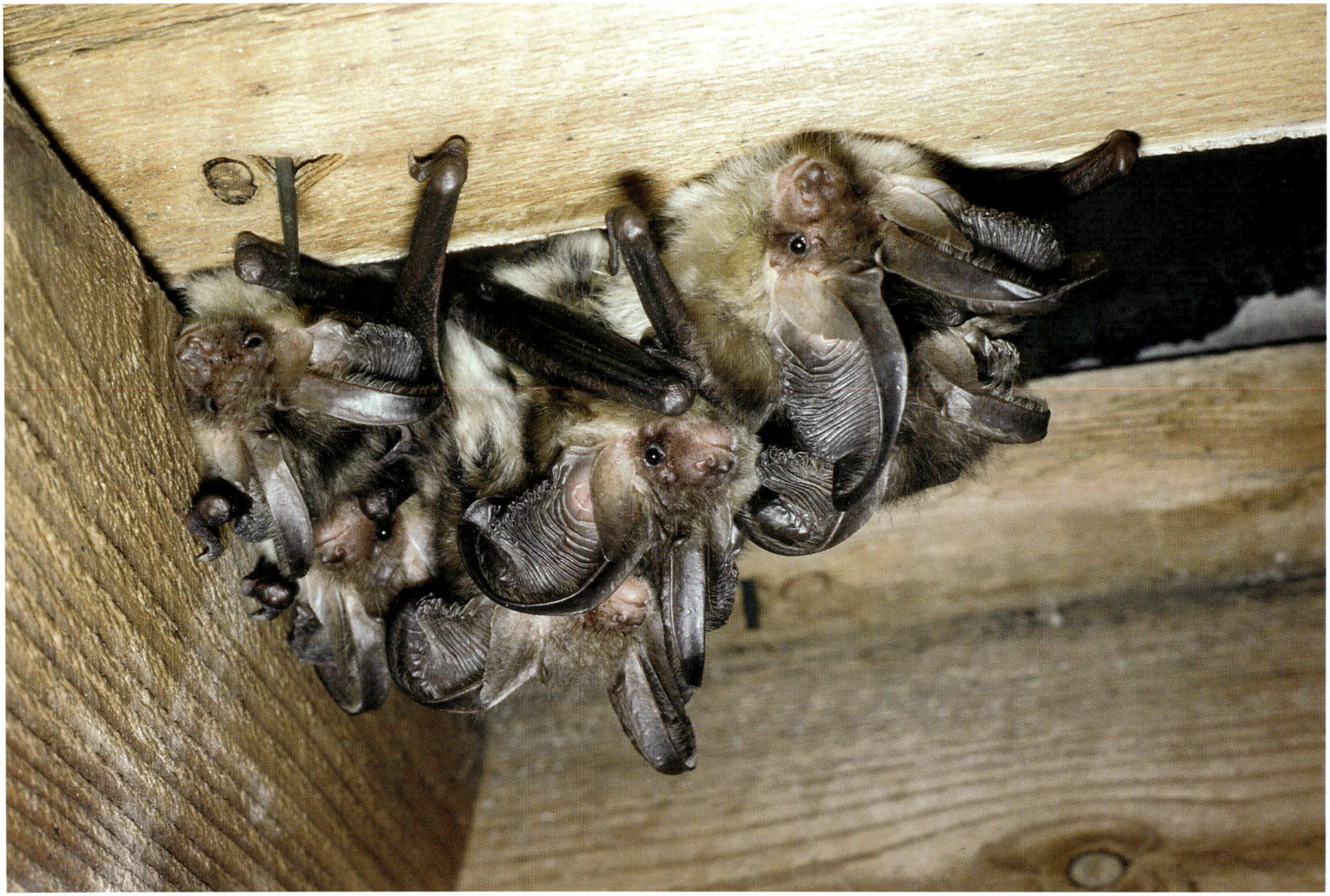

Like all nocturnal mammals bats can't see the red end of the visible spectrum. When faced with a conventional torch, the bats react by moving away from the light. But when the torch lens is covered with a piece of thin red plastic, we can still see the bats, but they are completely unaware of the dark red glow that illuminates them. Of course bats have other wonderfully acute senses that tell them what is happening, so it's important to keep sound to a minimum and move slowly. But I've found that visible danger seems to worry bats more than anything else.

These brown long-eared bats are roosting in the attic of a house in Herefordshire. Bats have an unfortunate reputation that is completely undeserved. Like all British species their numbers are steadily dropping. If you have resident bats of any species, cherish them. Bats have been on the receiving end of some truly dreadful publicity over the past few centuries and almost all has been totally misleading. Bats are gentle, intelligent animals that pose no threat to humans.

It's true that in South America there are bats that live off blood, but European species are insect-eaters. They don't transmit diseases or get caught up in human hair. Unlike rats and mice, bats don't gnaw through wire or contaminate humans' food. They eat many of the flying insects that most of us don't want in our homes. And, contrary to popular opinion, bats are not blind. They can see just as well as an average human. Unless of course they are faced with red light.

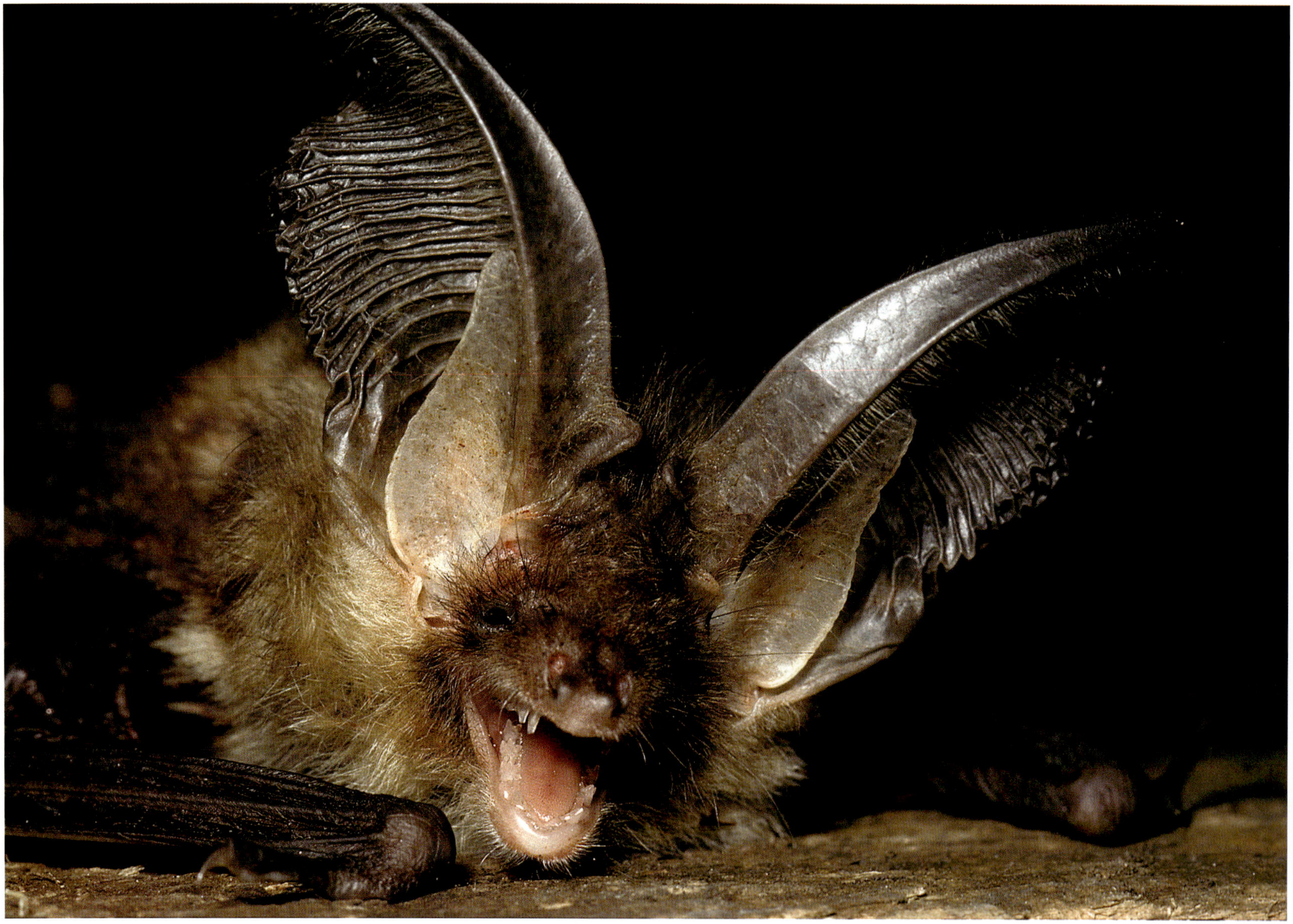

It's very easy to fuel people's prejudices and misconceptions by photographing only selective aspects of an animal's behaviour. The low camera angle and close-up approach of this portrait will be enough to make the susceptible feel very uncomfortable. The tight framing, side-lighting and dark background all contribute an extra feeling of menace to the overall scene.

I spent a long time with this long-eared bat and it showed no sign of fear or aggression. The tiny animal opened its mouth just once and only then for a moment. This picture is not an accurate record of the bat's behaviour. But if this is the only image you are allowed to see, it will colour your view of these gentle, harmless creatures. The camera can – and frequently does – completely manipulate reality.

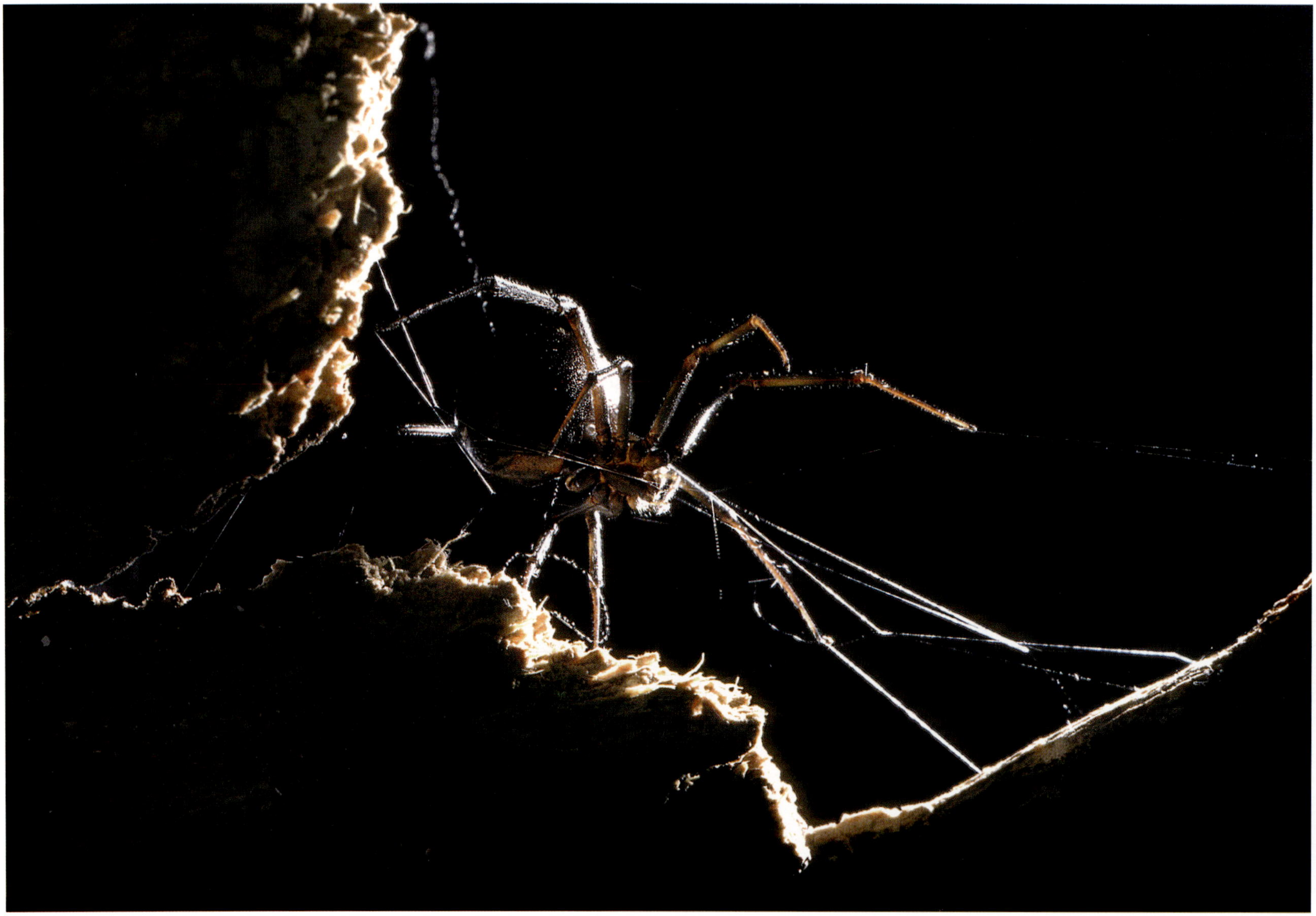

Dramatic lighting is an easy way of enhancing the atmosphere of a portrait, but it can be overdone and the approach is not appropriate for all animals. However, there are some species that thoroughly deserve to be shown as potentially dangerous and menacing – for the simple reason that they are both.

This black widow spider is about the size of my thumbnail. But it is one of the world's most poisonous animals. The black widow's venom is fifteen times more powerful than that of a rattlesnake. The poison is a potent neurotoxin that completely disrupts the nervous system. Within a few seconds of a bite, the pain is intense; thirty minutes later it is completely unbearable. The victim goes into violent spasms, sweats profusely and has difficulty breathing. Many bites are lethal.

Fortunately the black widow is a shy, docile creature that scuttles away when a human comes close. They rarely bite even under extreme provocation. You almost have to sit on a black widow before it will retaliate. That scenario is not as unlikely as it sounds. In remote corners of the USA, black widows are frequently found spinning their webs beneath the seats of outside toilets. You have been warned.

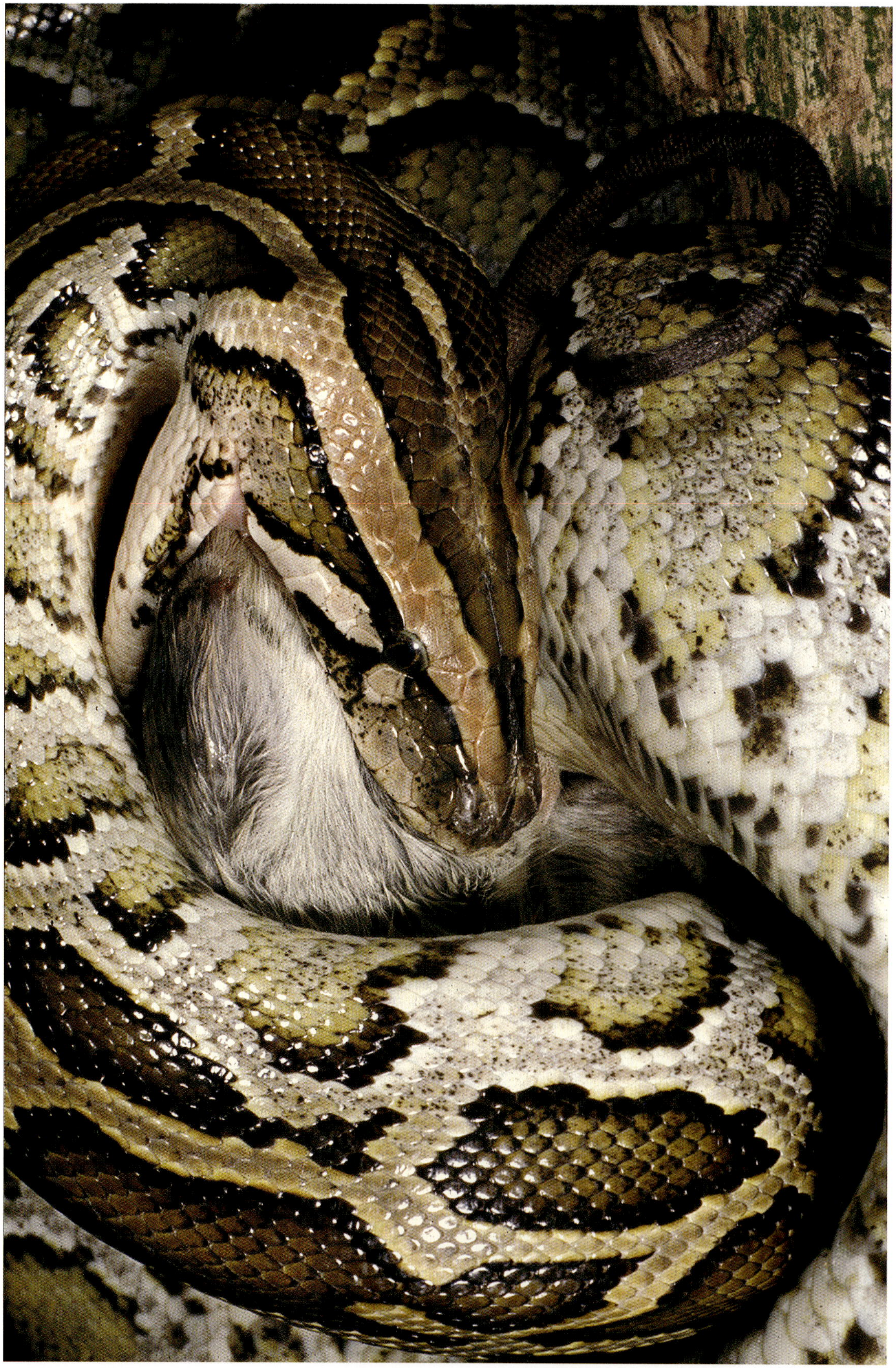

I'M FASCINATED by the way people respond to animals, because our reactions are emotional rather than intellectual. Psychologists have long known that most humans prefer animals that look most like humans. And that statement does make sense if you consider it for a while. People like animals that remind us of ourselves. We like creatures with an upright stance, two arms and two legs, and forward facing eyes. Which is exactly why koalas, penguins, pandas and owls always come top in the list of favourite animals. We are comfortable with that basic body design and anything that deviates too far from this familiar shape is slightly suspect.

This helps explain the complementary theory. Because, generally speaking, the animals we find least attractive are those that look least like us. Most people dislike spiders because they have too many legs. And most people don't like snakes because they don't have enough legs. Few of you will look at this picture of an Indian python objectively. Most will find it vaguely unsettling and some will quickly turn the page in search of something less offensive. I know perfectly well that this reaction is not a photographic criticism, it is simply an automatic response to the nature of the subject. We view animals with our hearts rather than our heads.

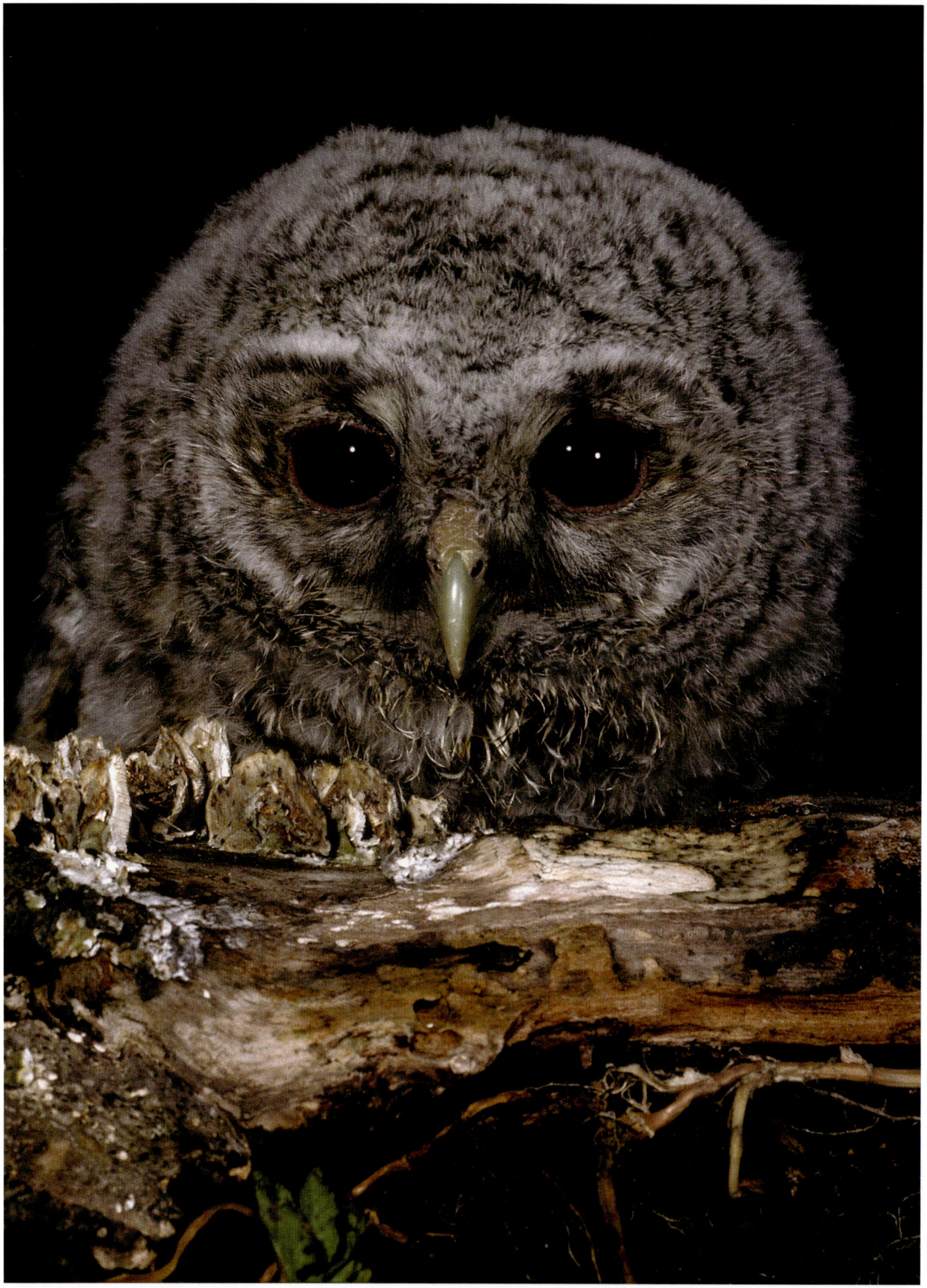

The ultimate antidote to all snake pictures.

Tawny Owl Chick aged three weeks | 55

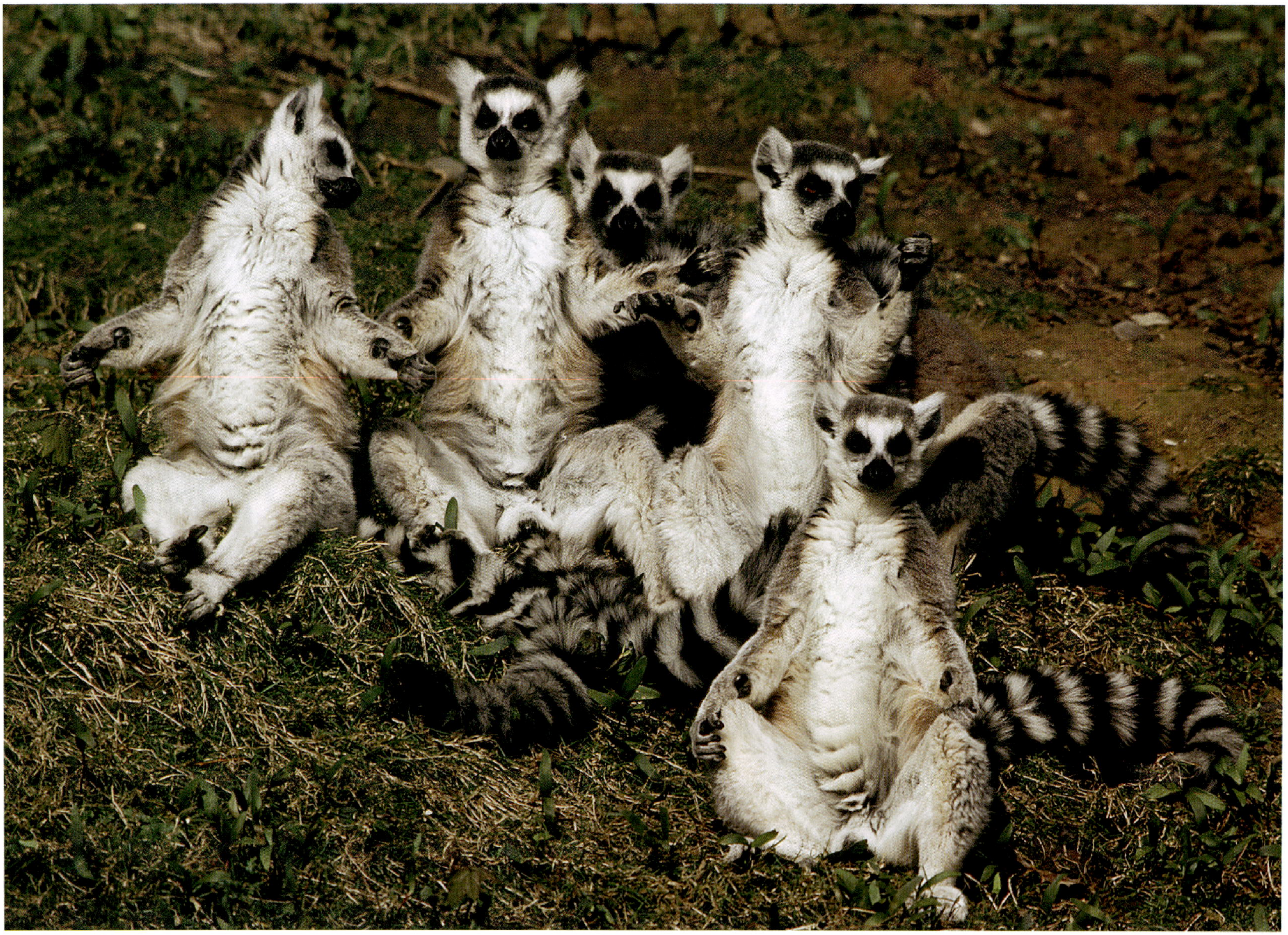

Madagascar is a huge island in the Indian Ocean off the East Coast of Africa. It has been separated from the rest of world for possibly 150 million years. This isolation allowed the island to explore its own evolutionary path and emerge today with a unique ecosystem. Madagascar is home to plants and animals that cannot be found anywhere else on Earth.

Amongst the weird and wonderful creatures that live on this beautiful island, lemurs are one of the most beguiling. Today around fifty species are known to science, but there may well be a few more tucked away in the remote wilderness areas that have yet to be fully explored by naturalists. Lemurs are members of the primate family: related to monkeys, apes and of course humans. Sometimes it's not too hard to see a connection between lemurs and man.

Ring-tailed lemurs are the most widespread species of their family. They are found throughout the south of Madagascar and often become very tame. Ring-tails are cat-size animals that roam the forest in groups, communicating to each other by flicking their distinctive tails in the air. Like us, they are omnivores that eat a wide variety of animal and plant food. But lemurs, in turn, are hunted by predators such as the Madagascar ground boa, a large snake that is active under the cloak of darkness.

Lemurs are particularly vulnerable at night, as their nocturnal vision is no better than our own. But they have evolved an efficient survival strategy: shortly before dusk the lemurs climb the tallest tree in the forest. They drape themselves over impossibly thin branches and go to sleep. A large snake is just too heavy to negotiate these heights, so the lemurs spend the night in peace and safety. There is just one problem. This may be the tropics but high in the tree tops, the lemurs are exposed and lose bodyheat during the night. By the time the sun rises the following morning, the animals are cold and need to warm up quickly. As soon as it is light enough to see, the lemurs clamber down from the trees and go off in search of heat. When they reach a patch of sunlight, their reaction is stunningly familiar. I find it impossible to look at this scene without being reminded of human holidaymakers. *Homo sapiens* isn't always as unique and sophisticated as we like to think.

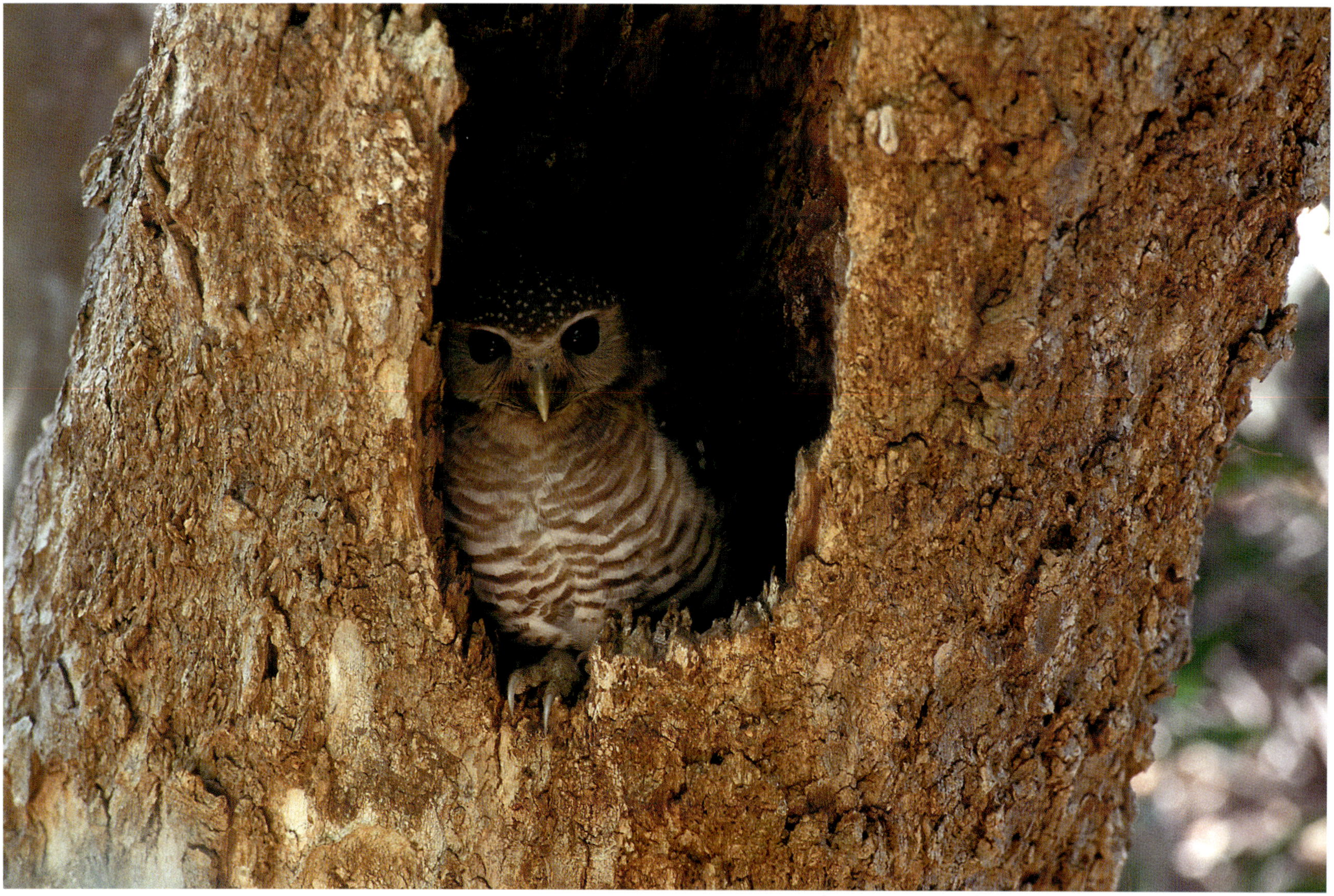

Wherever I'm working in the world, I always try to find time to go on an owl hunt. It's a hit-and-miss business but there's always the chance of finding something completely new, particularly when exploring a new country. Having spent nearly a week with the ring-tailed lemurs, I took a day off and went in search of Madagascar's owls. I looked in every nook and cranny, scanned the likely roosting sites and wandered huge chunks of forest. All I found were yet more ring-tailed lemurs and lots of unidentified bugs; there was no sign of an owl, neither a feather nor a pellet. It was a complete failure.

It was back to work with my lemurs the next day and I was in the forest at dawn. But as the group left the tree tops it soon became obvious that they had changed their normal early morning routine. The lemurs left their usual feeding ground and entered an unfamiliar area of forest. They made a beeline for a huge tamarind tree that was ripe with seed pods. The lemurs collected fallen pods from the ground and then cracked open the long seed cases to reach the rich food inside. After taking a few rolls of film of this new behaviour, the lemurs were still enthusiastically feeding so I started to investigate my surroundings and came across an ancient hollow tree. In the decomposing trunk, at head height, there was a small hole out of which came a series of soft scratching sounds. I scratched back and waited. A few seconds later out popped one of the prettiest faces I've ever seen. It belonged to a female Madagascar hawk owl, a species not found anywhere else.

The owl sat in the entrance of the hollow tree and blinked lazily. This was a good sign; owls show stress by increasing their blink rate. This one was unperturbed by the sight of a human. After a couple of minutes her eyelids drooped and she slowly drifted off to sleep. A couple of minutes was all I needed.

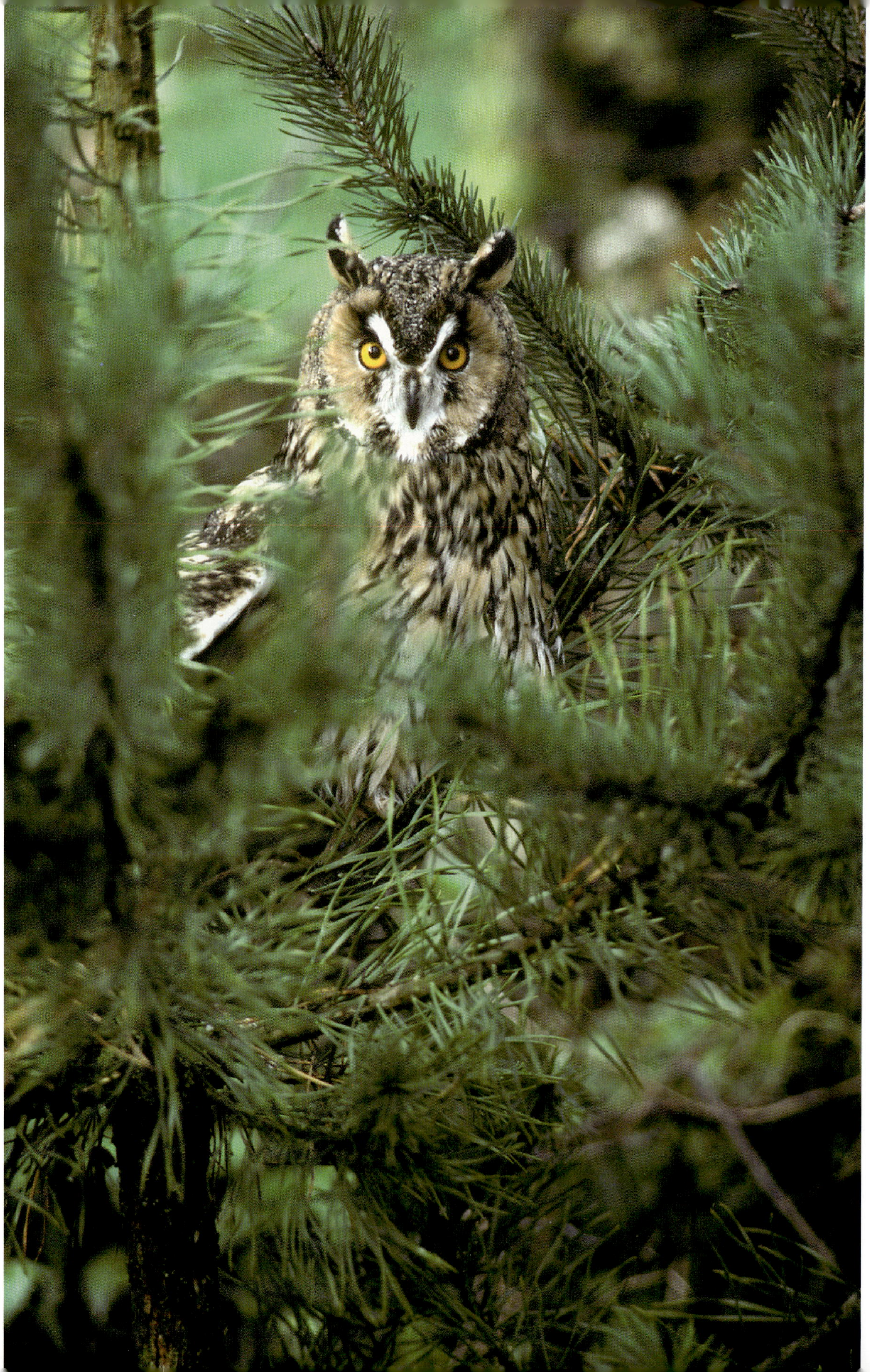

Owls are one of my favourite subjects. Like almost everyone else I'm drawn by both their magnetic appearance and their vaguely supernatural qualities. There are around 135 species of owl living in the world today and I'm slowly working my way through the list. It's depressing to realise that some will probably be extinct before I ever get the chance to see them.

Of the five breeding species in Britain, I find the long-eared the most fascinating. Although not particularly uncommon, these birds are very rarely seen. They are intensely shy animals and, unlike many other owls, they never live close to human habitation. Very few people have a chance to see a live, wild long-eared owl.

Even when accidentally wandering close to a long-eared owl roosting in a quiet woodland, we usually walk by without noticing. These owls have a wonderful ability to blend into their surroundings. At the first sight of a human, they freeze and just become part of the tree. There's a real art to finding owls; it involves 'tuning-in' to their appearance and knowing exactly where to look. It takes a while to master but eventually owls can be seen in places where, previously, there were none.

The owls' freezing technique makes life easier for wildlife photographers. Instead of immediately vanishing, as most birds do, owls simply sit motionless in the absolute conviction that they cannot be seen. Incidentally, the name 'long-eared' owl is highly misleading. The distinctive tufts on top of the head have nothing to do with ears, they are simply long feathers – nothing else. An owl's ears are invisible; they are tucked away under the feathers on each side of the skull, just behind the eyes.

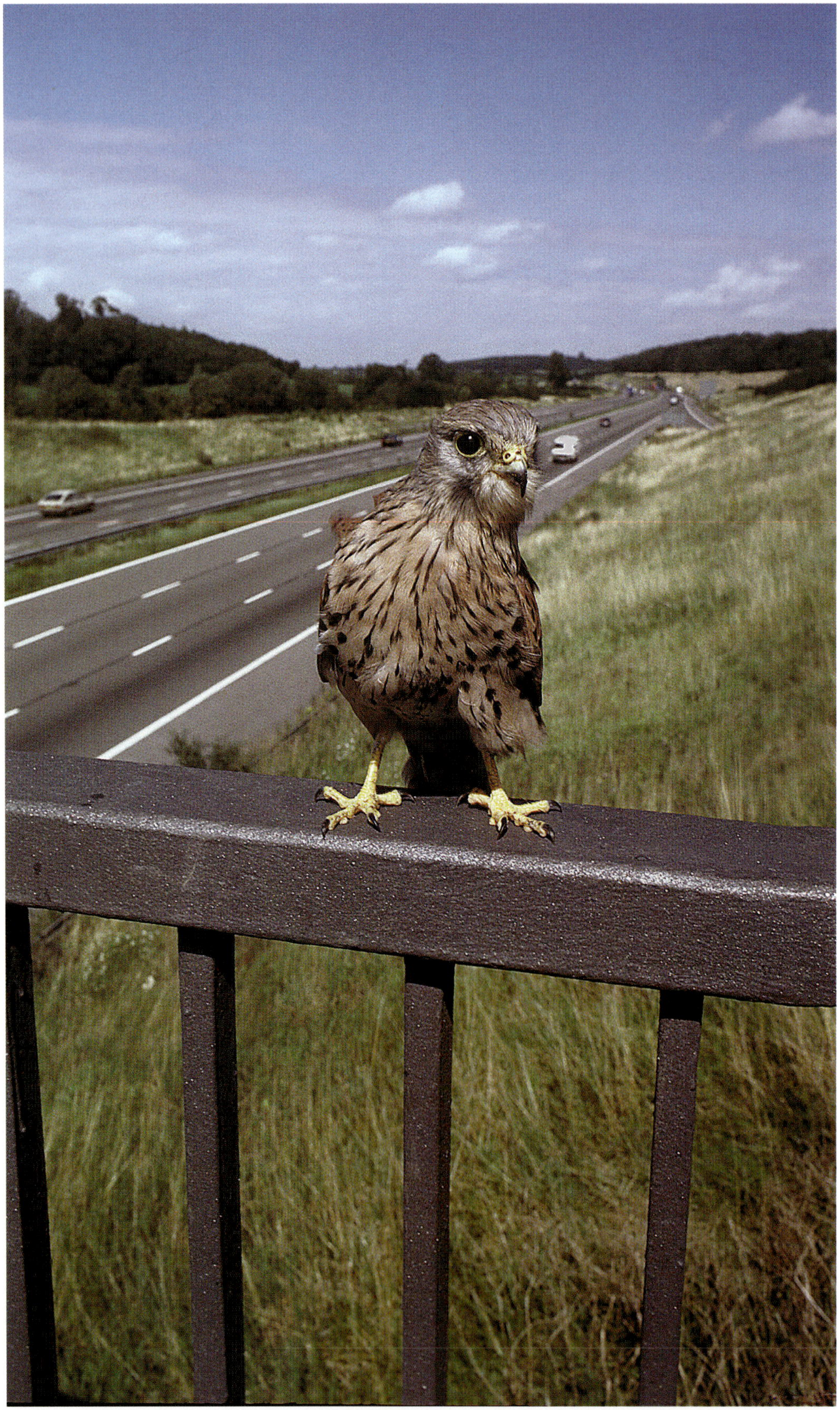

In the late 1950s kestrels were rapidly becoming an endangered species in Britain, due mainly to the effect of some particularly unpleasant agricultural pesticides such as DDT. Then two totally unconnected events occurred that completely altered the fortunes of the kestrel. The pesticides were banned and motorways were introduced.

Motorways were designed to relieve the growing pressure on small roads and provide quick, efficient routes for motorists travelling long distances. What no one could possibly have predicted was the effect motorways would have on local wildlife. Obviously road construction on this scale caused a huge amount of environmental damage to existing habitats. Meadows, woods and hedgerows were destroyed to make way for the sterile tarmac; but the building programme wasn't a total disaster for wildlife.

The endless narrow grassy verges were created as buffer zones to separate the traffic from the surrounding landscape. But they quickly became home to a huge number of insects, reptiles and small mammals. As the verges became established and the vegetation grew more diverse, other animals moved in and slowly an entirely new habitat was born. The motorway verge system is now a long thin interconnected corridor containing an astonishing number of species. It's illegal to park on a motorway, so humans never disturb these animals. No one walks their dog, or has a picnic, or plays football. Once the animals have learned to accept the proximity of traffic, they are free from the influence of people. Weasels, lizards, grasshoppers and hedgehogs now make their home in this unique environment. And, hurtling by at 70 mph, drivers never suspect what is happening inside the narrow green blurs alongside the road.

The only visible sign of the motorway's hidden wildlife are the distinctive silhouettes of hovering kestrels that float high above the roaring traffic. These elegant falcons are searching for the mice and voles that scuttle amongst the wind-blown grass, unseen by us but clearly visible to the kestrel's acute eyesight. With a sudden stoop the bird drops into the undergrowth and seizes another meal in its powerful talons. On average each mile of motorway has its own resident kestrel. Today they have become so familiar that we just don't really notice them any more. But next time you see a kestrel, remember that it is just the tip of the iceberg. You won't see the other animals that surround you – but they are there.

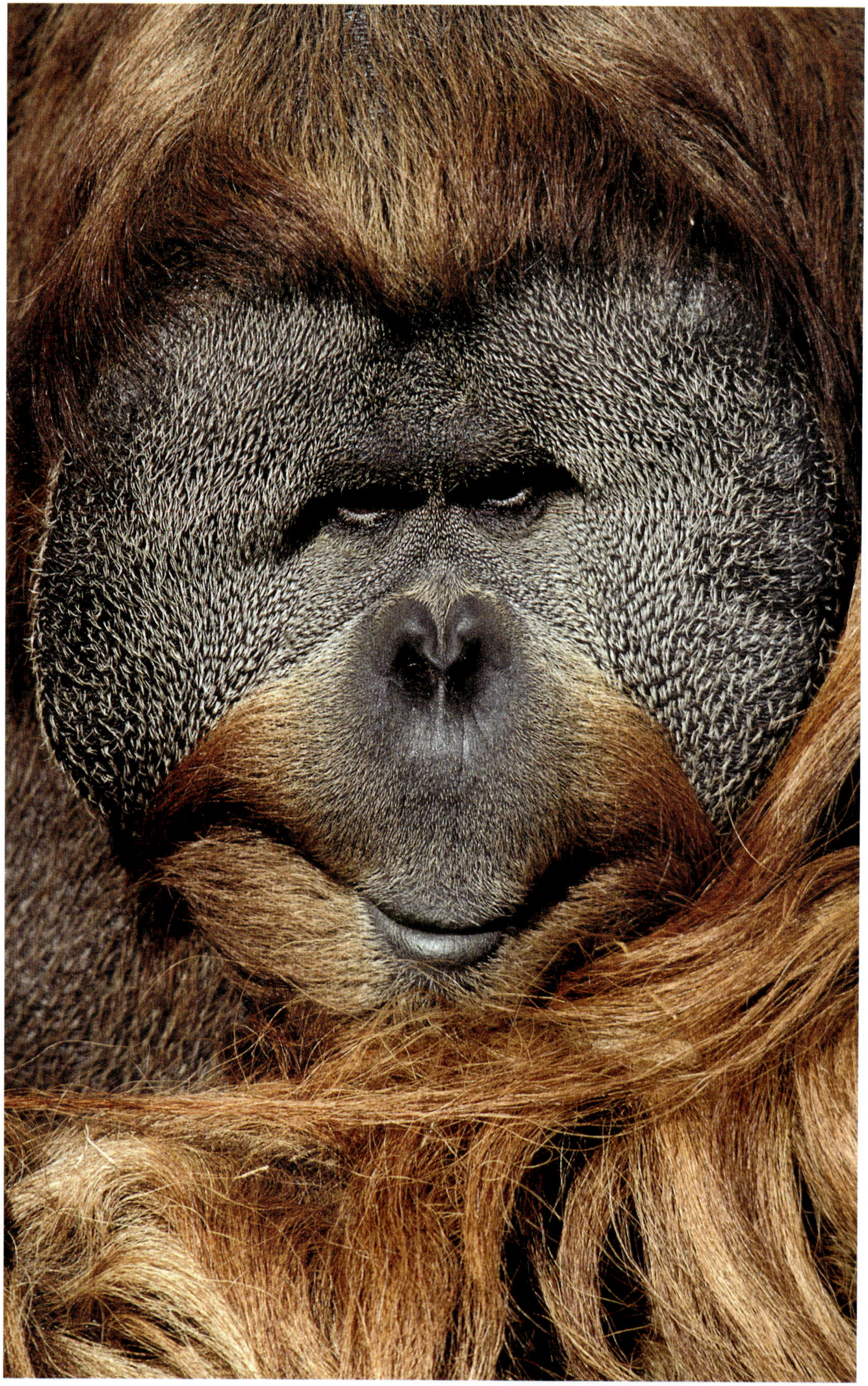

Some photographs simply need no words.

Male Sumatran Orang-Utan

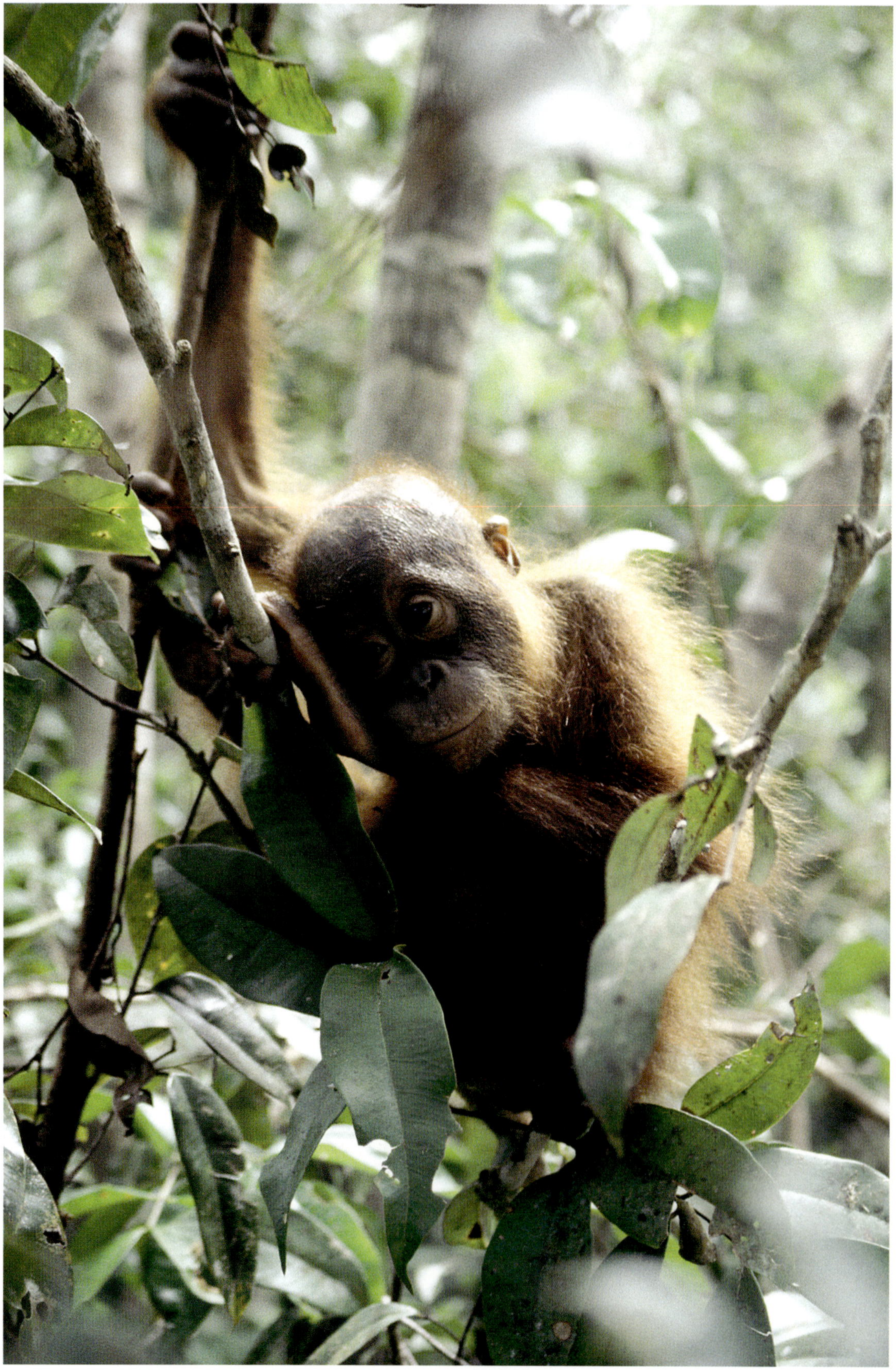

Of my countless early mistakes, one of the most naïve was the idea that once I had taken a few decent pictures of an animal then the species had been 'done' and it was time to move on to something new. It didn't take long for me to realise that this was a completely ridiculous concept. Most animals lead lives that are so complex and diverse that we cannot even begin to understand the subtleties of their behaviour. They constantly adapt to new habitats and learn different skills. Each individual has its own character that is shaped by unique surroundings and experience. These elements can significantly affect their lives and, sometimes, may be reflected in photographs.

Orang-utans, together with gorillas, chimpanzees and bonobos, are our closest living relatives. These are the great apes. I once spent three years writing and illustrating a book on these clever, inventive, sentient, curious animals. Only when it was finished did I realise that it would be impossible to produce a definitive collection of photographs of the great apes – even after a lifetime's work. These animals are simply too sophisticated to be captured totally on film. The best we can hope for is to record a small cross-section of their existence. The previous page shows a conventional portrait of a dominant male in his prime, the picture opposite is of the same species but it bears a totally different message.

This three-year-old female orang-utan was photographed in a rehabilitation centre. No one knows the exact story but around two years earlier a poacher had gone into the forest and shot her mother. There is a vile black market trade in baby orang-utans, which is supplied in the most barbarous way. Orang-utans have to be captured young if they are to have any resale value and the only way to catch one is to kill the mother first. The terrified baby would then have been sold as a pet or side-show attraction and kept under horrific conditions. This particular young ape was covered with scars and had a broken arm when she was found wandering along a road in Taiwan.

At that age she should still have been with her mother; instead she has been brutalised and exposed to the very worst of human behaviour. It's hardly surprising that a portrait of this orang-utan is very different from that of the animal on the previous page.

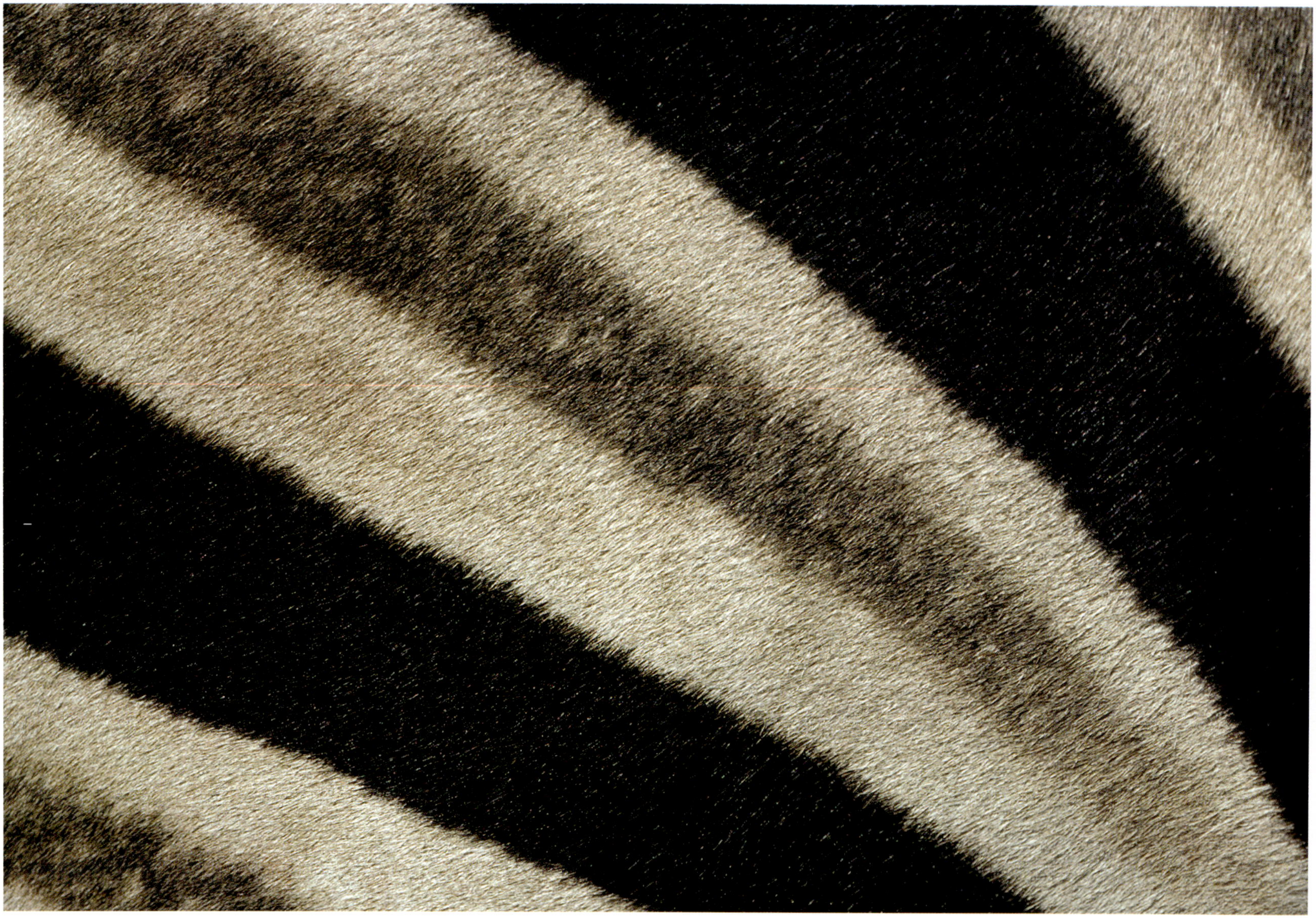

Some animals are so familiar and so terribly over-photographed that it is difficult to come up with new images. Zebras are one of the archetypal creatures of the African plains, they live in huge herds that wander the savannah; visible for miles they are no challenge to the wildlife photographer. Zebras don't even bother to look up when approached by a tourist bus in a busy National Park. Even totally inexperienced visitors on their first safari take home a small mountain of zebra photographs. There is no point adding to this vast collection.

To produce something different it is sometimes necessary to take a close look at iconic animals to try and work out their essence. What single picture can capture and distil the spirit of the beast? With zebras that question is easily answered.

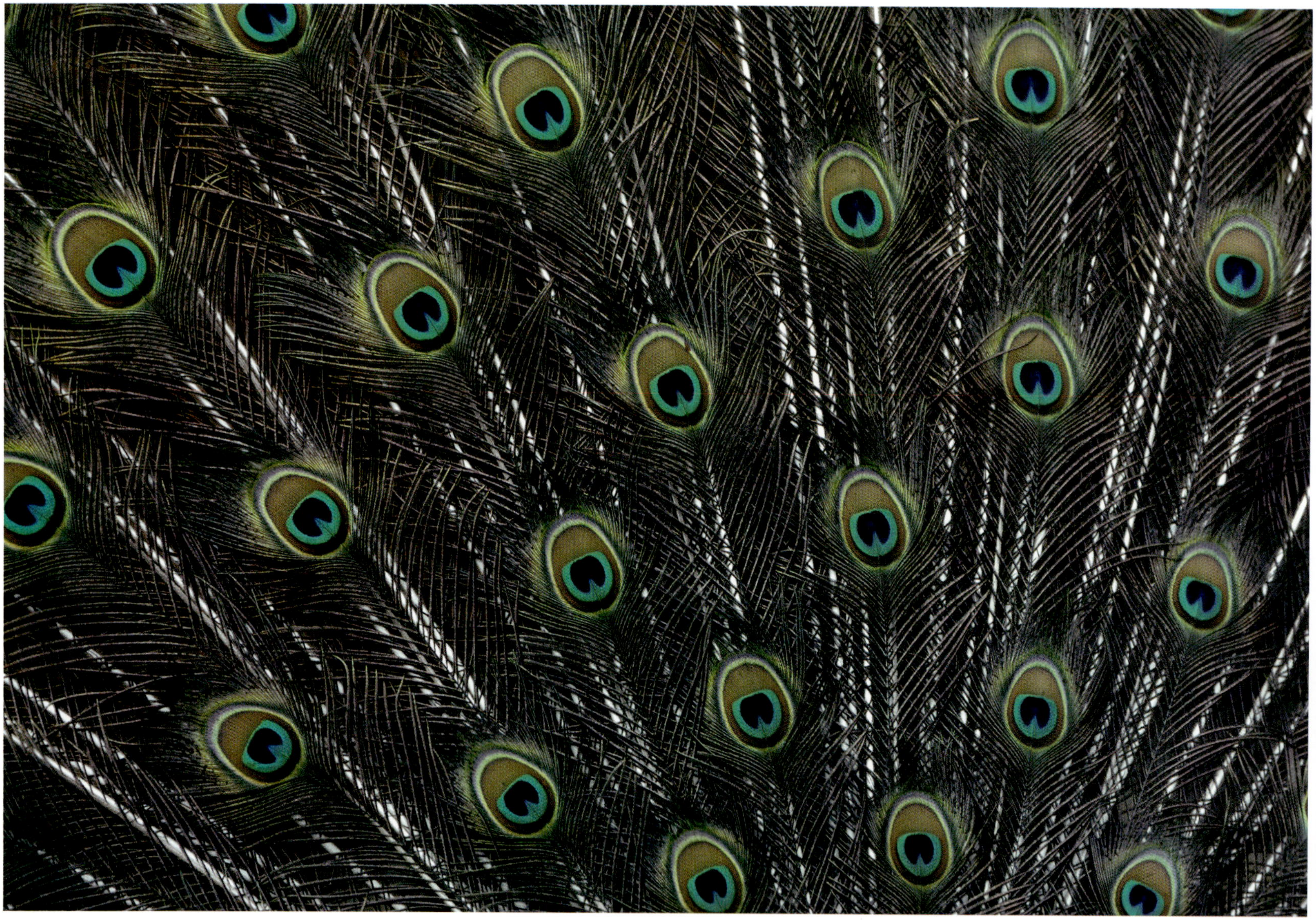

Only male peafowl sport these flamboyant and unmistakable tail displays. And they only reveal them at certain times of the year. Yet these eye-patch feathers are about the only anatomical detail that most people know of peafowl. Very few can recall the colour of the birds' eyes or how many toes they have.

The quivering, vertical display of outrageously long and brightly coloured tail feathers must be the most recognisable sight in the bird world, even to those that know nothing about wildlife. This picture doesn't need any other information. Our experience and imagination fill in the gaps.

Although peafowl are now seen in almost every park, zoo and stately home in the world, their original home is in the forests of India. They may be aloof and confident in a British park but in their native habitat peafowl are shy birds that are rarely seen. They have excellent hearing and eyesight, senses that allow them to keep well away from humans. This is a good survival strategy as peafowl are regularly hunted for food by big cats, wild dogs and humans.

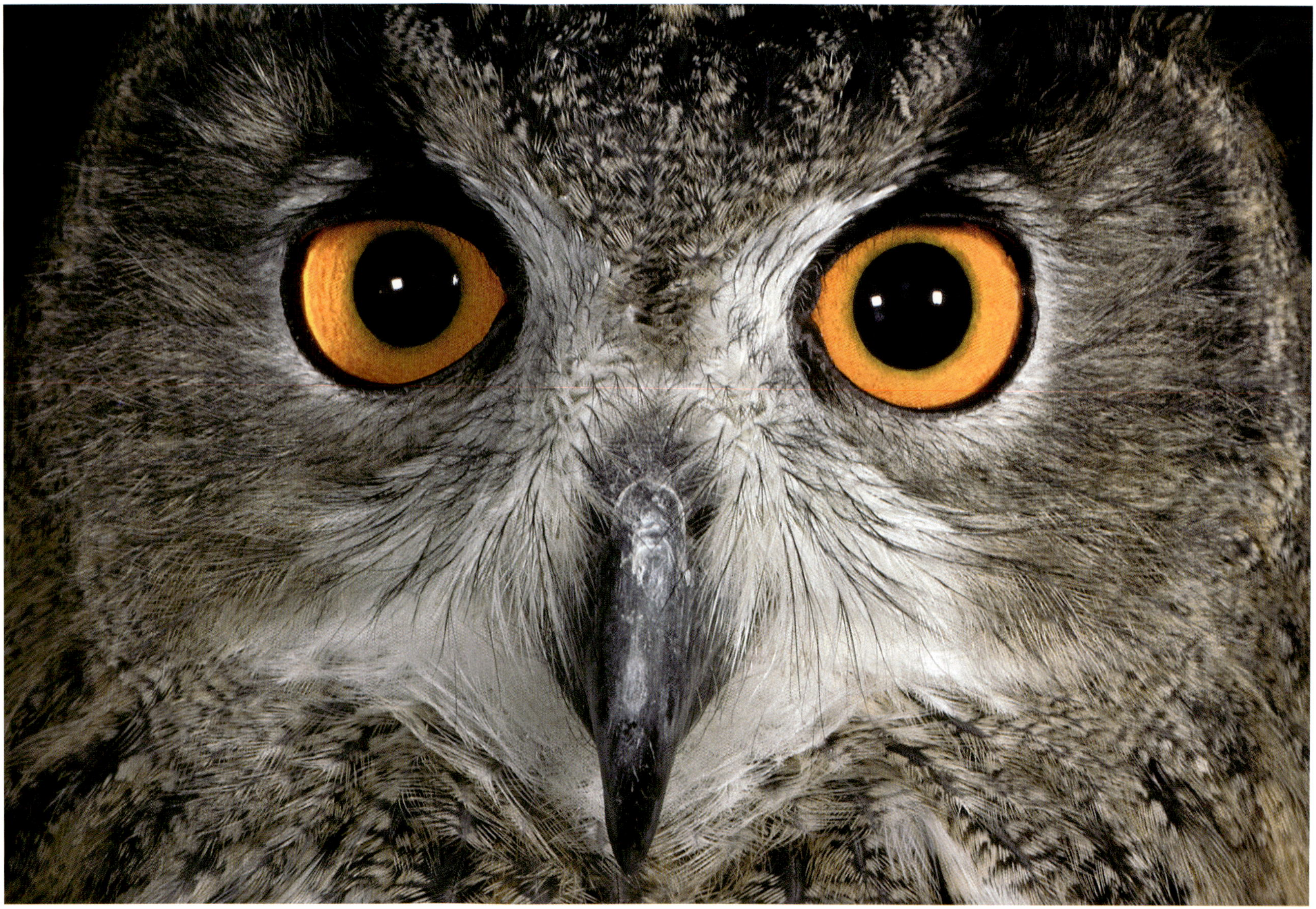

SOME ANIMALS have such natural photogenic qualities that there is no need to use sophisticated camera techniques or arrange elaborate backgrounds. The European eagle owl must surely have the most magnetic eyes of any creature on Earth. No photographer could possibly improve upon the intrinsic charisma of such extraordinary eyes – and it would be foolish even to try. There are times when we must accept that it is simply enough to aim the camera at the right place and allow the animal to do the rest.

The startling orange colour of this owl's eyes has nothing to do with its sight. These extraordinary eyes are vivid warning signals to other animals, telling them to keep away or suffer the consequences. The European eagle owl is the largest owl in the world. They are formidable hunters that prey on animals as large as roe deer. As in most owl species, the female is noticeably larger than the male; they have a wingspan that is equivalent to the span of my outstretched arms. In their natural habitat adult eagle owls are at the top of the food chain, they have no enemies apart from, inevitably, humans. Eagle owls were once found over most of Europe, including Britain, but over-hunting almost completely wiped them out. Today they live in the wilderness areas of Scandinavia and just a handful of other sites in the rest of Europe.

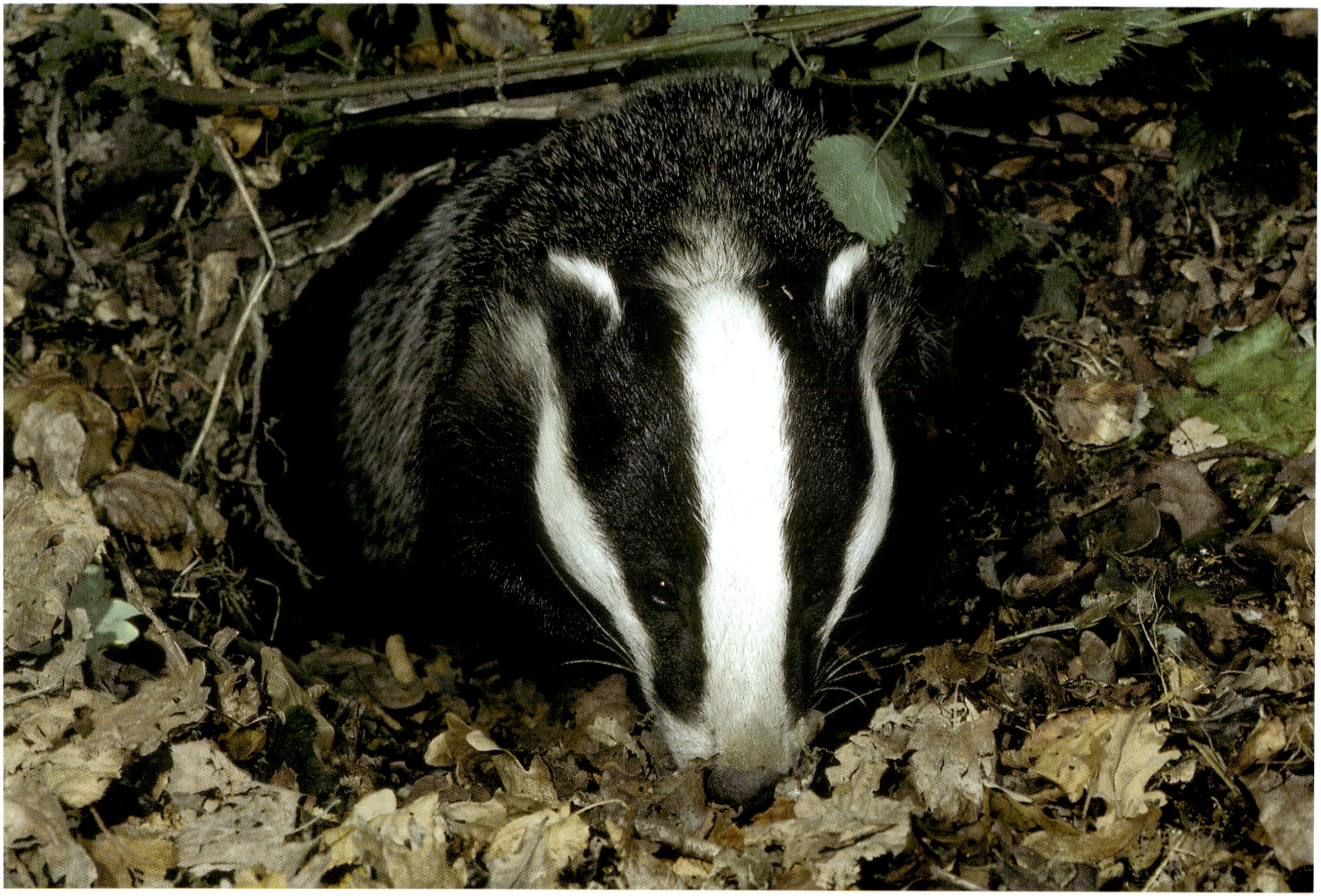

The badger's distinctive black-and-white striped face serves the same purpose as the eagle owl's eyes. They are a highly visible warning sign that tells the unwary to back off. Badgers are peaceful animals that may look slow and cuddly, but they are extremely powerful and perfectly capable of defending themselves against any predator.

Badgers are nocturnal; they spend their days sleeping in underground dens at the end of tunnels that can be twenty metres long. The sleeping chambers are warm and dry, each is lined with fresh grass that the badgers change every few days. Badgers are quite short-sighted but they have an excellent sense of smell. Before venturing into the outside world at sunset, each animal stands just inside the den entrance and sniffs the air, checking for signs of possible danger. If all is well, the badger trots out and immediately begins to search for the earthworms that make up the bulk of its diet.

Like the vast majority of mammals, badgers have a sweet tooth. They crave sugar, a commodity that is hard to find in the British countryside. Devious wildlife photographers can use this to their advantage. A few hours before the badgers are due to come out, we hide a handful of sultanas and chocolate drops in the leaves at the den entrance. This must be done quickly and delicately, to ensure that we don't leave the intimidating scent of humans behind as well. When the badger appears at dusk, he will pause at the entrance to scent the air, he will also detect the smell of food. For a few minutes the badger stands at the entrance nosing through the undergrowth eagerly looking for his unexpected treats.

The camera has already been set up and focused on that precise spot and the badger is too interested in the food to take any notice of the distant clicks and whirrs.

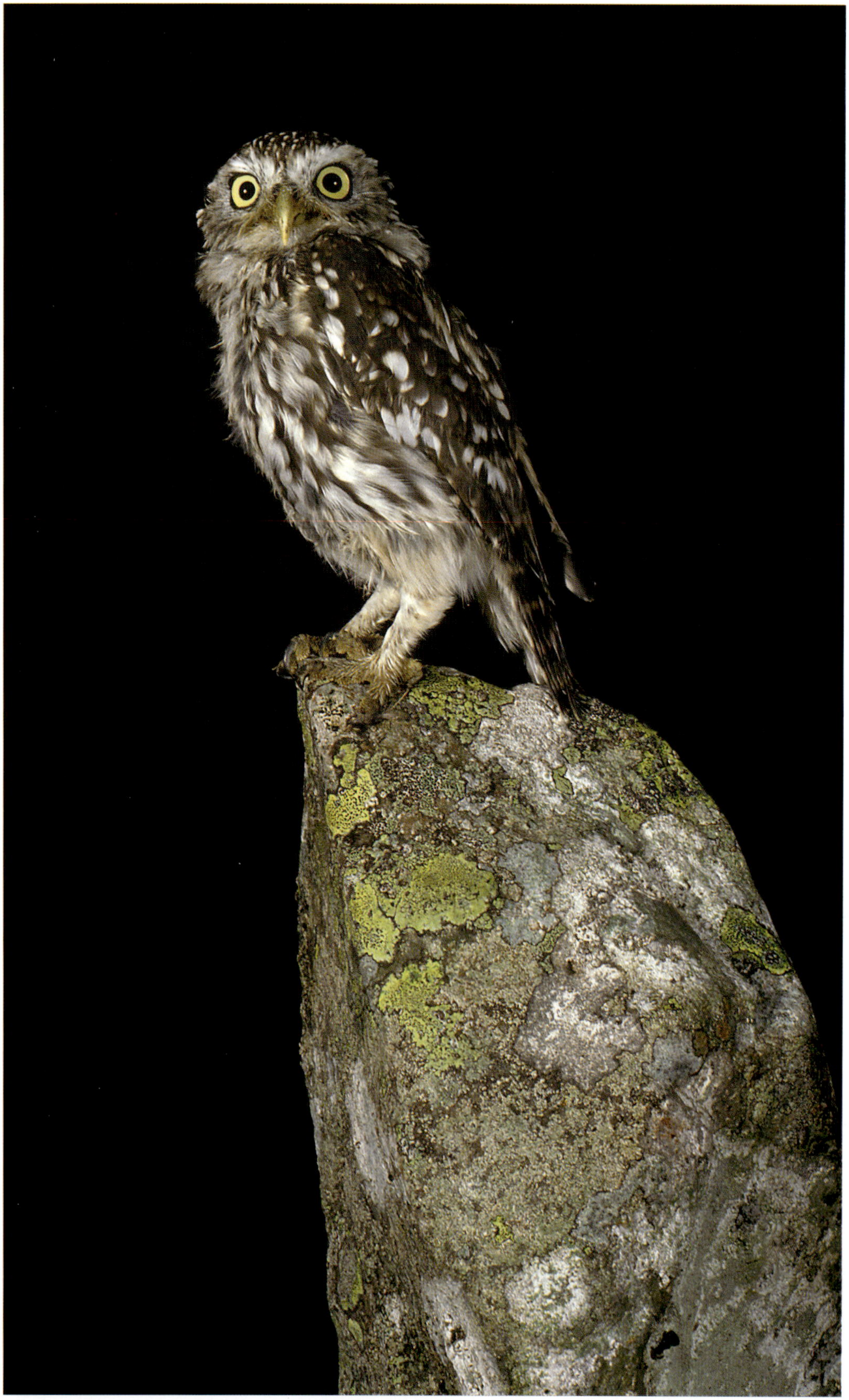

SUCCESS sometimes lies in the detail. I found this lichen-covered rock by chance and thought it would make a wonderful prop in a picture. But it was a long time before the opportunity arose to use it to the best effect. A robin or blackbird would have been wasted on this beautiful boulder. The scale would have been wrong and the combination of colours would never have worked.

But a little owl was perfect. The size and camouflage of the bird exactly suited the rock. And the fact that it was a nocturnal animal allowed me to use flash and turn the background inky black.

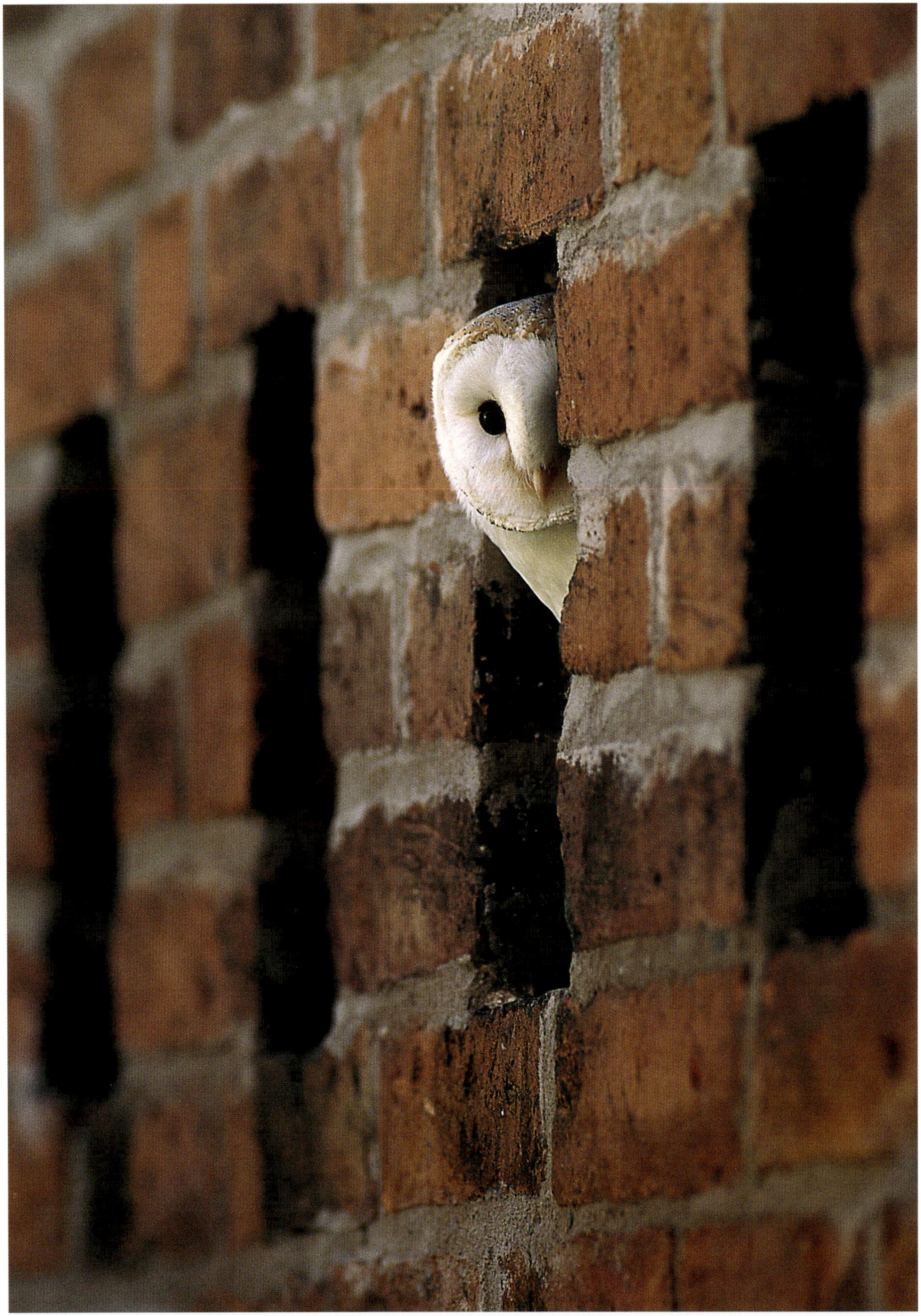

THE OWL was in exactly the right place – doing something wonderfully interesting, at just the moment when I was holding a camera. This is pure luck.

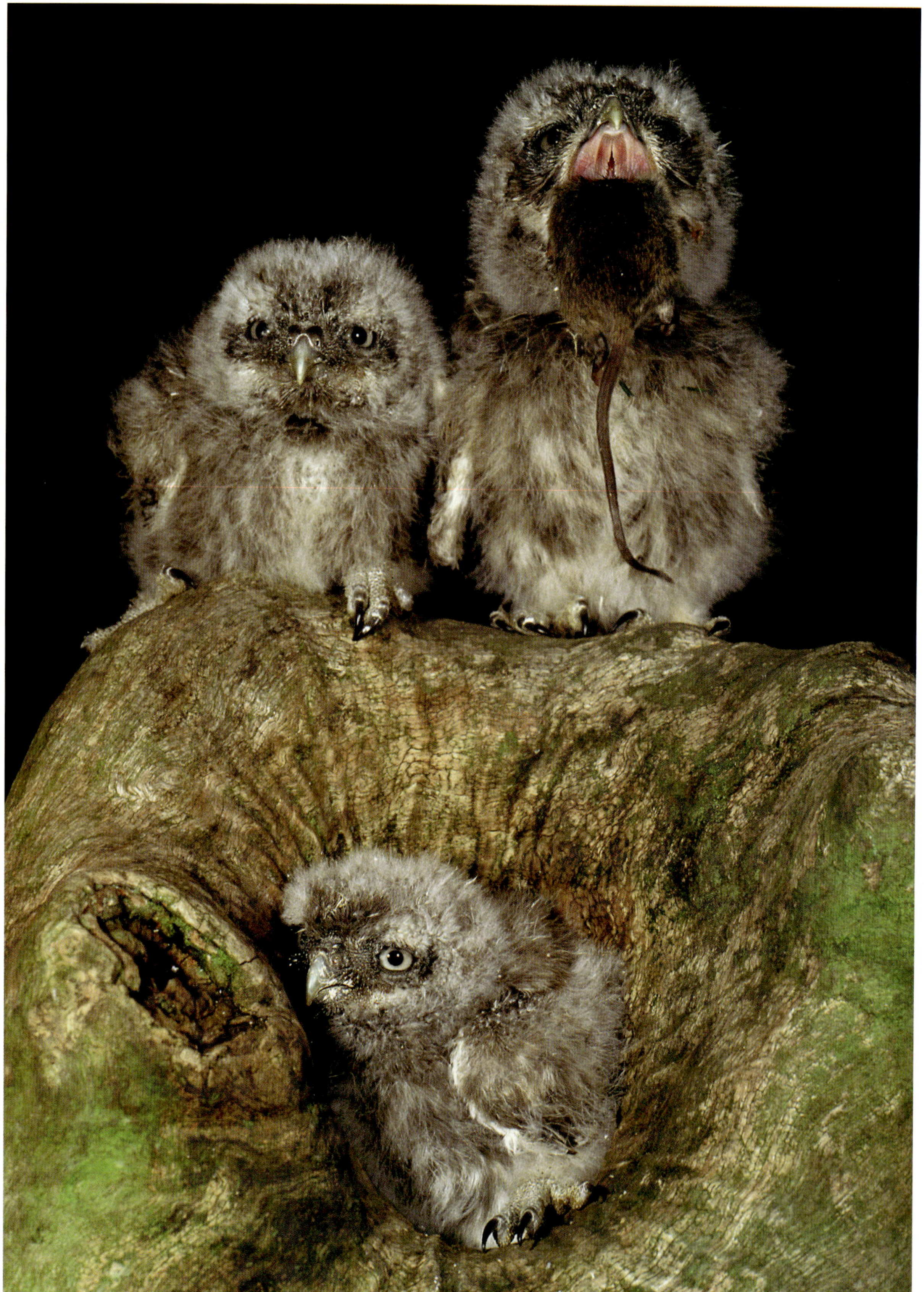

Wildlife photography consists largely of doing nothing. Exponents sit waiting endless hours, for that fleeting moment when the animal turns up or does something interesting. In the back of my mind there is always a rough list of the pictures I need. Sadly, the animals never see the list and plans rarely turn out as expected.

But just occasionally something completely unexpected takes place. This picture only works because the little owl chick sitting on top of the stump is attempting to swallow a mouse that is exactly the same length as its own body. It was a titanic struggle and, for a while, it was touch and go. But after a long, determined struggle the owl eventually triumphed and the mouse disappeared. The owl was rewarded with the biggest meal of its short life and I went home with a unique set of photographs.

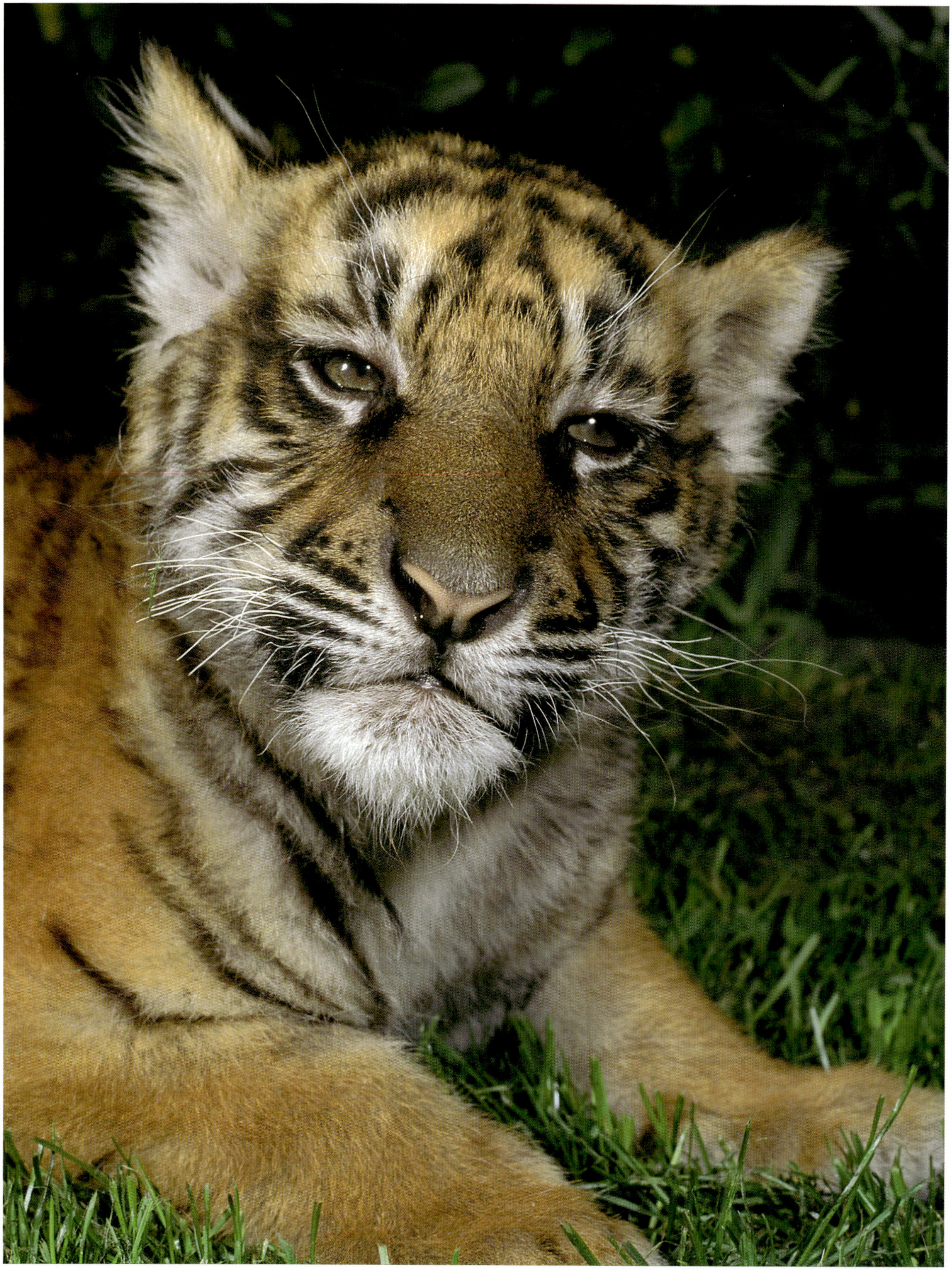

The Bengal tiger is now breathtakingly rare. It's quite likely that less than 800 tigers are left in the wild. Just 100 years ago there were more than 100,000 roaming the forests of Asia. Humans are the sole cause of the tiger's destruction; we have shot them, trapped them and wiped out their habitat. If wildlife photography has any worthwhile role, it is to remind people that tigers, and hundreds of other species, are destined for extinction unless we do something. If we continue to relentlessly exploit the natural world we will casually wipe out the animals that we all find so fascinating.

At least our generation still has the chance to look and wonder at some of these rare species. Our children won't be so fortunate – by the time they are grown many of these animals will have disappeared. There'll be none left to see. And the blame can be fairly laid at our feet.

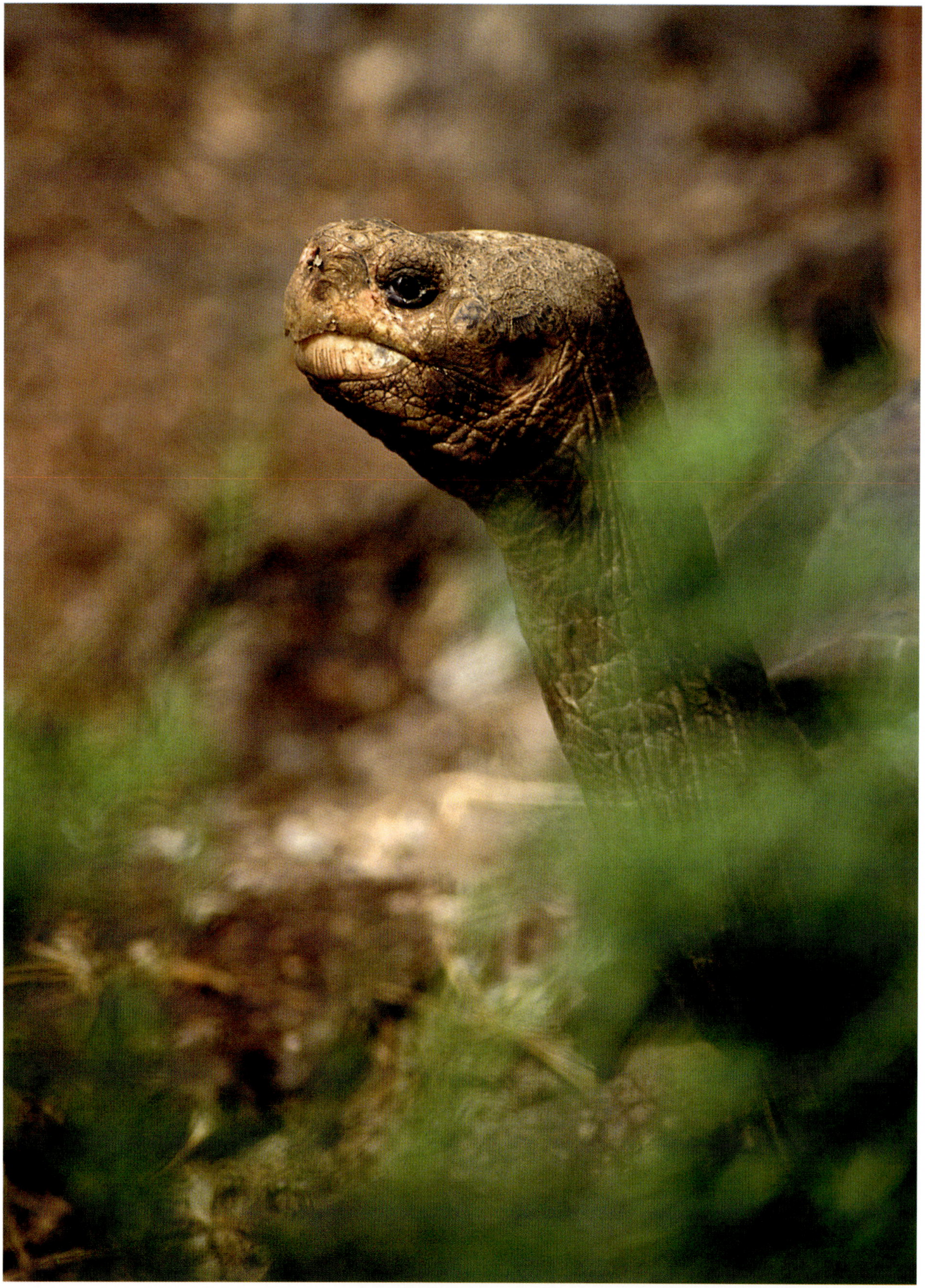

This animal belongs to a race that is absolutely, irrevocably condemned to extinction, for the simple reason that he is the last of his kind left alive. 'Lonesome George' is the sole survivor of the giant tortoises that once thrived on Pinta, one of the Galapagos Islands. Each of the major islands originally had its own individual sub-species of tortoise; Isabella, the largest island, had five distinct races. Every population was unique and found nowhere else, and each race was distinguished by the shape of its shell.

The first Europeans came to the Galapagos in 1535 and found a tortoise population that was measured in tens of thousands. Giant tortoises are huge, an adult weighs up to 136 kg and to a protein-hungry crew of sailors, tired of eating fish and dried biscuits, these exotic animals were an irresistible food supply. Some were killed on the spot and their meat was dried and salted. Many more were captured live and kept aboard ship until needed. Even without food or water giant tortoises can live for up to a year in these conditions. One captain reports that he once loaded 14 tons of live tortoises for a single trip in the 1820s. Over four centuries an estimated 200,000 giant tortoises were slaughtered. Eventually the population levels fell so low that ships no longer stopped, there simply weren't enough tortoises to make it worthwhile.

Pinta had been terribly exploited. No giant tortoise had been seen on the island since 1906, they were assumed to be extinct. Then in 1972 a group of scientists arrived to study goats but were astounded to find a single ancient tortoise. Despite extensive searches, no other tortoise has ever been found on Pinta. As a precaution George was moved to a large compound at the Charles Darwin Research Station on the Island of Santa Cruz.

There is a $10,000 reward currently being offered to anyone who can produce another live Pinta tortoise. None have been found. At the time of writing this race of giant tortoise was the rarest animal on Earth. But soon that dreadful accolade will have been transferred to another unfortunate creature. It is difficult for me to imagine a more moving and powerful argument for conservation.

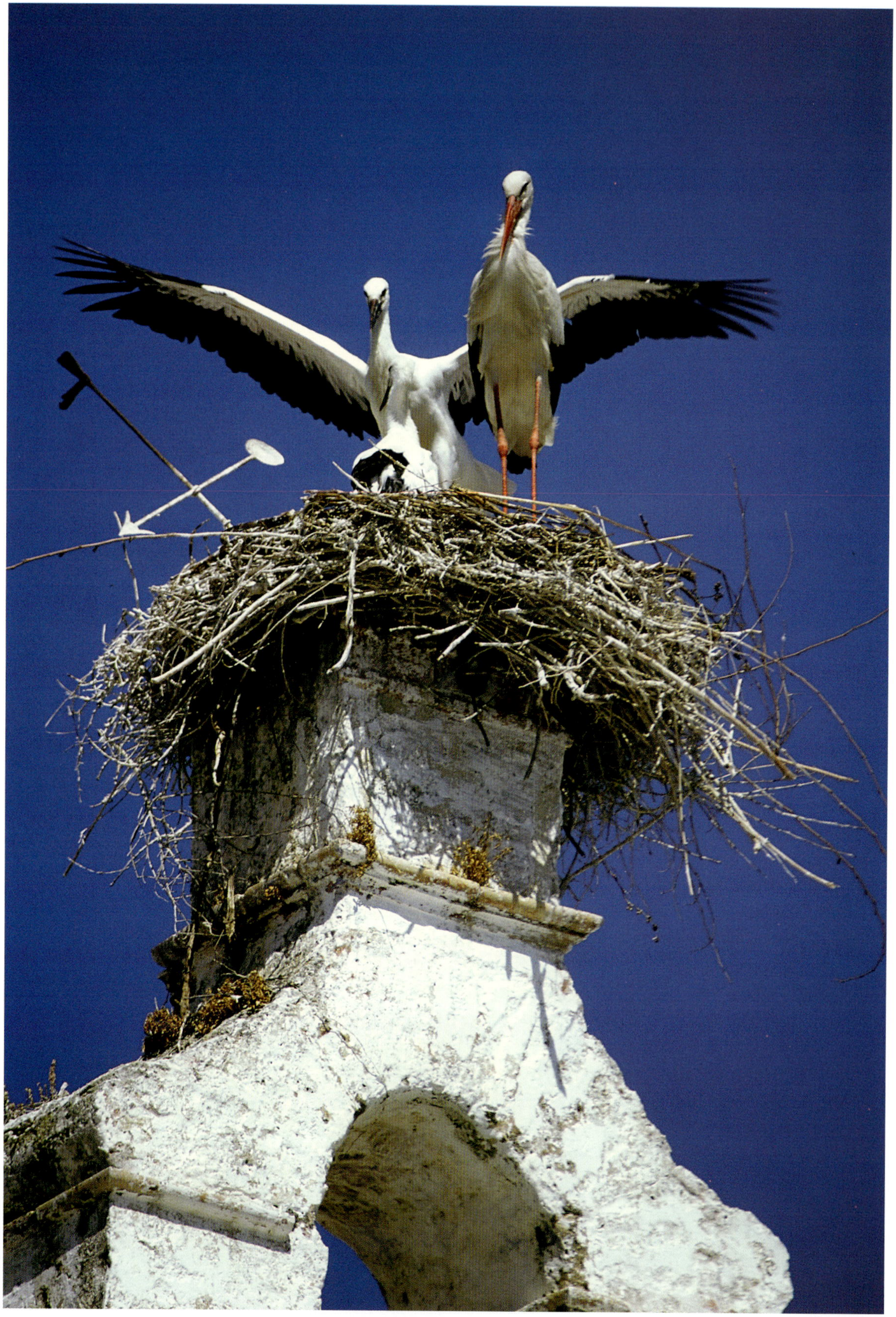

One hot July day, after spending a week photographing wildlife in the Guadalquivir estuary in Spain, I drove from El Rocío on the west coast to Málaga Airport on the Mediterranean. It wasn't a long trip and there was plenty of time to enjoy the scenery, as the route over the mountains was tortuous but wonderfully picturesque. It was one of those remorseless, oven-like Spanish summer days. Nothing moved and when the sun reached its highest point, the car became just too hot to tolerate. It was time to take a break and, in a tiny mountain village, a shady tapas bar beckoned.

I sat beneath a huge, ragged parasol, sipping freshly squeezed orange juice and nibbling an assortment of unidentified food from small bowls. The village was no more than a single square and a few side streets. It was dominated by an old whitewashed church, and in the intense sunshine the walls were almost too bright to look at. Balanced on top of the bell tower was a tangled mound of untidy twigs, meticulously put in place by a pair of white storks. Standing on this heap were two huge stork chicks. The youngsters were fully grown, but they hadn't yet developed the distinctive bright red beak and legs of the adults that ferried in the food supply every few minutes.

The storks weren't difficult to spot. They stood on the tallest building in the village, frantically flapping their wings. Every few minutes each chick rose fractionally in the air before inelegantly dropping back down into the nest. The car was parked next to the tapas bar so fortunately I didn't have to go far to collect my equipment. With an orange juice in one hand and a camera in the other, I spent a delightful afternoon taking photographs. The sky was impossibly blue and the waiter was attentive.

By mid-afternoon the sun had dropped beneath the ridge of a nearby hill; the church was in shadow and I had a plane to catch. Twenty-four hours later the stork chicks would have left, having abandoned their nest and taken to the hills to begin an independent life. The week on the Guadalquivir hadn't been wildly successful – unlike my three hours in the tapas bar.

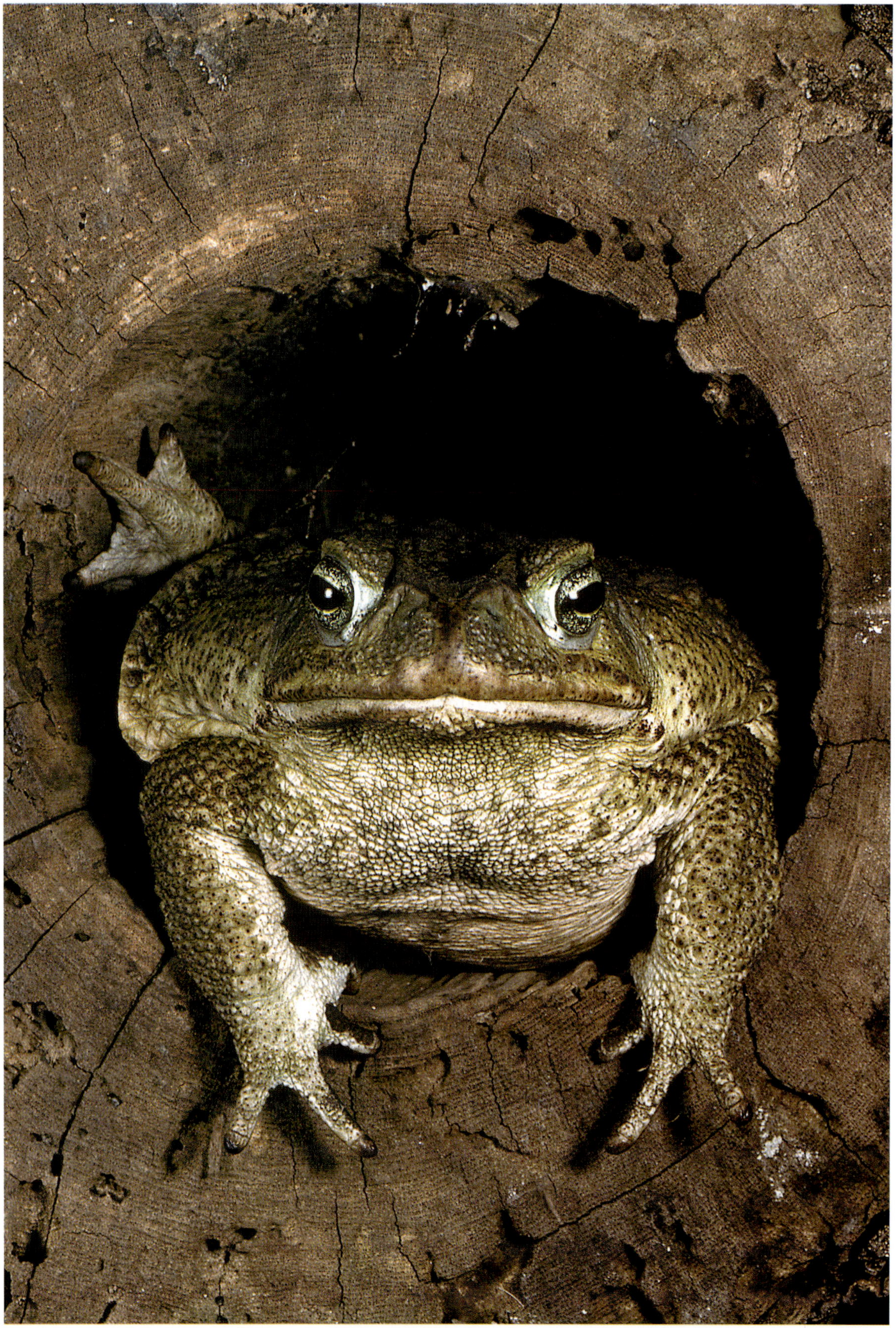

Marine toads are amphibians on a truly magnificent scale. Every biological fact about these creatures is impressive. A large female is about the size of a football and lays an unbelievable 30,000 eggs in less than a day. Their rough skin is so tough and durable it can be tanned and turned into shoe leather. They live in tropical rain forests, suburban gardens, ditches, sugar fields, reservoirs and almost any other warm wet habitat.

Marine toads originally came from the forests of South America, rather than the sea, as their name would suggest. Thanks to intentional introduction into many far-flung countries, the marine toad now has the widest global distribution of any amphibian. They have survived and thrived for two very good reasons. They have prodigious appetites and will eat insects, reptiles, small mammals and almost any other creature that will fit into their cavernous mouths.

But the real key to their success is a wonderfully refined self-defence mechanism. These giant toads cannot sprint or defend themselves conventionally. They appear to be an easy meal for any hungry predator. But if a jaguar or ocelot decides that marine toad is on the menu, it is in for an unpleasant shock. When the toad is frightened or stressed, tiny droplets of a thick milky liquid are released from the skin pores. This secretion tastes truly disgusting and can make a predator very ill. A single lick or tentative bite is enough to deter any enemy. The toad is dropped unharmed and the predator learns never, ever, to try eating one of these beasts again.

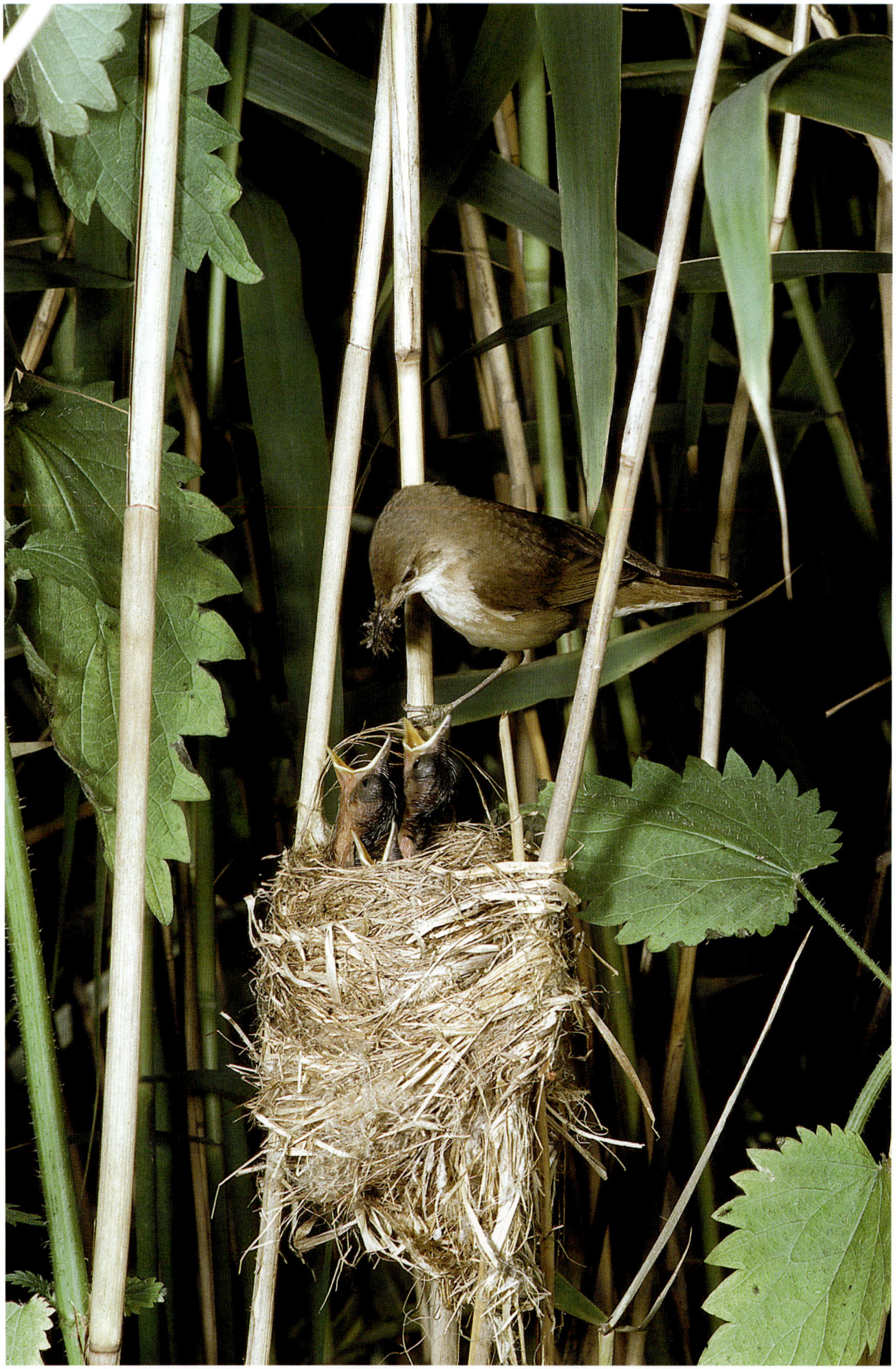

Wildlife photography is just as governed by trends and fashions as any other field. Styles and tastes come and go – only to return a few years later.

For decades nest behaviour was regarded as the ultimate form of portraiture. Birds are extremely protective towards their nests and are deeply wary if any large animal approaches – particularly humans. It would be completely impossible to stand by a nest and take pictures such as the one opposite; the birds would simply never come back while such a terrifying predator was close. Wildlife photographers must adopt a far less threatening appearance to get close to a nest. So we use hides, portable canvas boxes that are camouflaged to blend into the surroundings.

A hide is deliberately kept as small as possible, but it is still a lot bigger than the birds themselves. We have to persuade the birds that the strange construction is not dangerous by introducing it very slowly. On the first day the hide is built 10 metres away from the nest, and every day it is moved slightly closer. Over the course of a week the hide slowly creeps forward and the birds have plenty of time to look at it, think about it and eventually accept it as a natural part of their surroundings. When the hide reaches its final position, the birds treat it as simply another part of their surroundings. I've lost count of the number of times I've sat inside a hide while the owner of the nest is sitting on top.

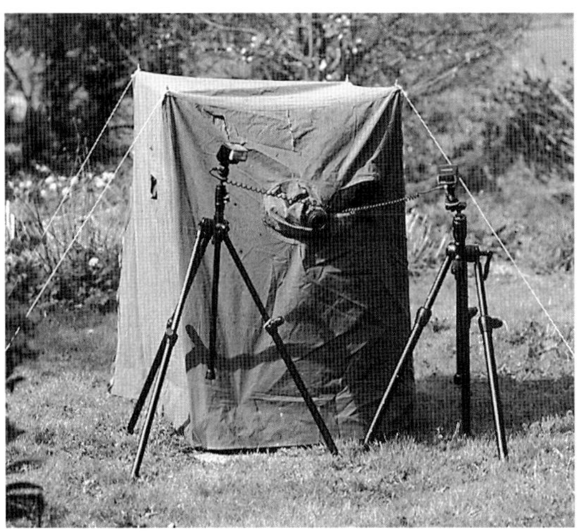

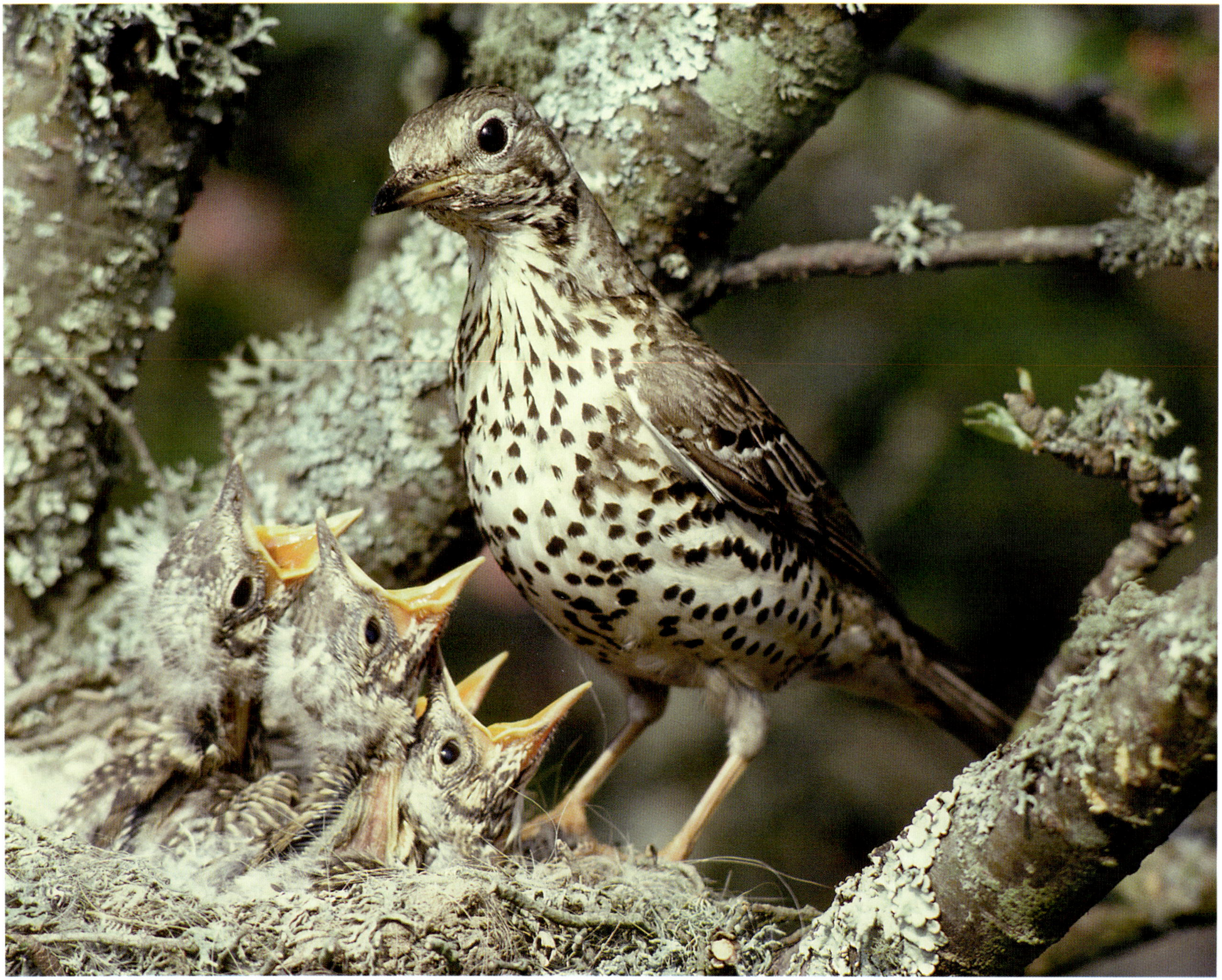

Mistle thrushes are one of Britain's earliest nesting birds; they are often sitting on eggs before the leaves are fully out on the branches around them. The mistle thrush has the distinction of having possibly more dialect names than any other bird. Jeremy Joy, Crakle, Big Mavis, Mizzly Dick and Skirlock are just some of the local terms for this highly distinctive bird.

For me, at least, the most appropriate is 'stormcock' because, unlike most birds, the mistle thrush seems to relish bad weather. In the spring when wind is howling through the treetops during an April squall, other birds find a sheltered hideaway and wait for better conditions. But the stormcock sits on the highest branch and gives out its long, raucous call. It is a very dramatic scene.

This picture illustrates the importance of timing. The adult thrush has just arrived back with food and each of the chicks is straining to be fed first. This is the moment to take the picture. Ten seconds later the meal will have been shared out and the chicks, knowing that their chance has now gone, will collapse into a tired heap until next time. Food may only arrive three times an hour, and on each occasion there are just two or three available seconds to get the right shot. If opportunities are restricted to eight seconds an hour, you can't afford to miss many.

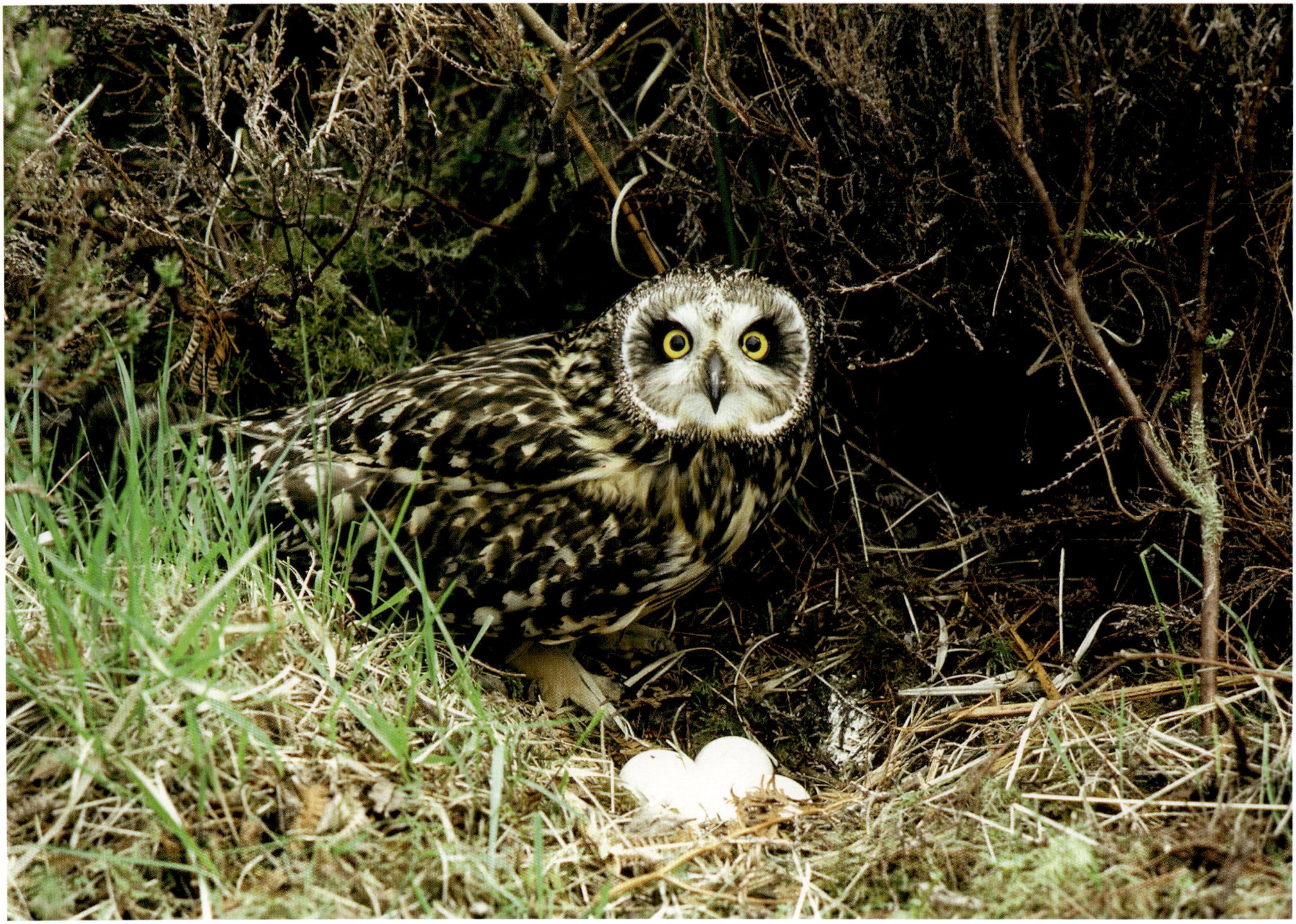

This short-eared owl was nesting on a remote hillside a long way from human habitation. Short-eareds are wary creatures and I had to be very careful not to do anything that might arouse its suspicions. I sat inside a hide just two strides away from the nest and did not move for thirteen hours. For some extraordinary reason people seem to think that wildlife photography is glamorous and exciting. Anyone under this misleading delusion should try squatting in a canvas box, slightly smaller than an armchair and infinitely less comfortable, for thirteen hours. While never forgetting – the whole time – that the animal in front does not know anyone is watching. So you cannot do anything that might make a sound and betray your presence. No singing, coughing, shuffling, eating crisps, no radios or magazines – no moving at all. But, and this is deadly serious, the real key to using a hide is not to drink anything before going in.

I conscientiously obeyed all the rules that day. No sound and no movement. But from the moment I entered the hide until the moment I left the owl did not take its eyes off the camera lens. Owls have long been associated with extraordinary eyesight but few people realise that they have equally acute hearing. Some species can hunt in absolute blackness, using only the sound of faint rustles to pinpoint the exact whereabouts of a mouse as it pushes through the undergrowth.

It is well known that an owl can keep its body still and rotate its head up to about 300 degrees. Conversely they can keep their heads still and rotate their bodies. No matter where the bird sat, its piercing mustard-coloured eyes were fixed on me. For the first time ever I felt as if the roles were reversed. Theoretically I was there to observe the owl, not be on the receiving end of a detailed scrutiny. The short-eared owl did not know it was being watched by a human but it was aware that something slightly strange was going on. It was a totally still day, with not even the slightest whisper of a breeze. The owl had been alerted by the sound of my breathing. A mere human can do nothing when faced with such well-developed senses.

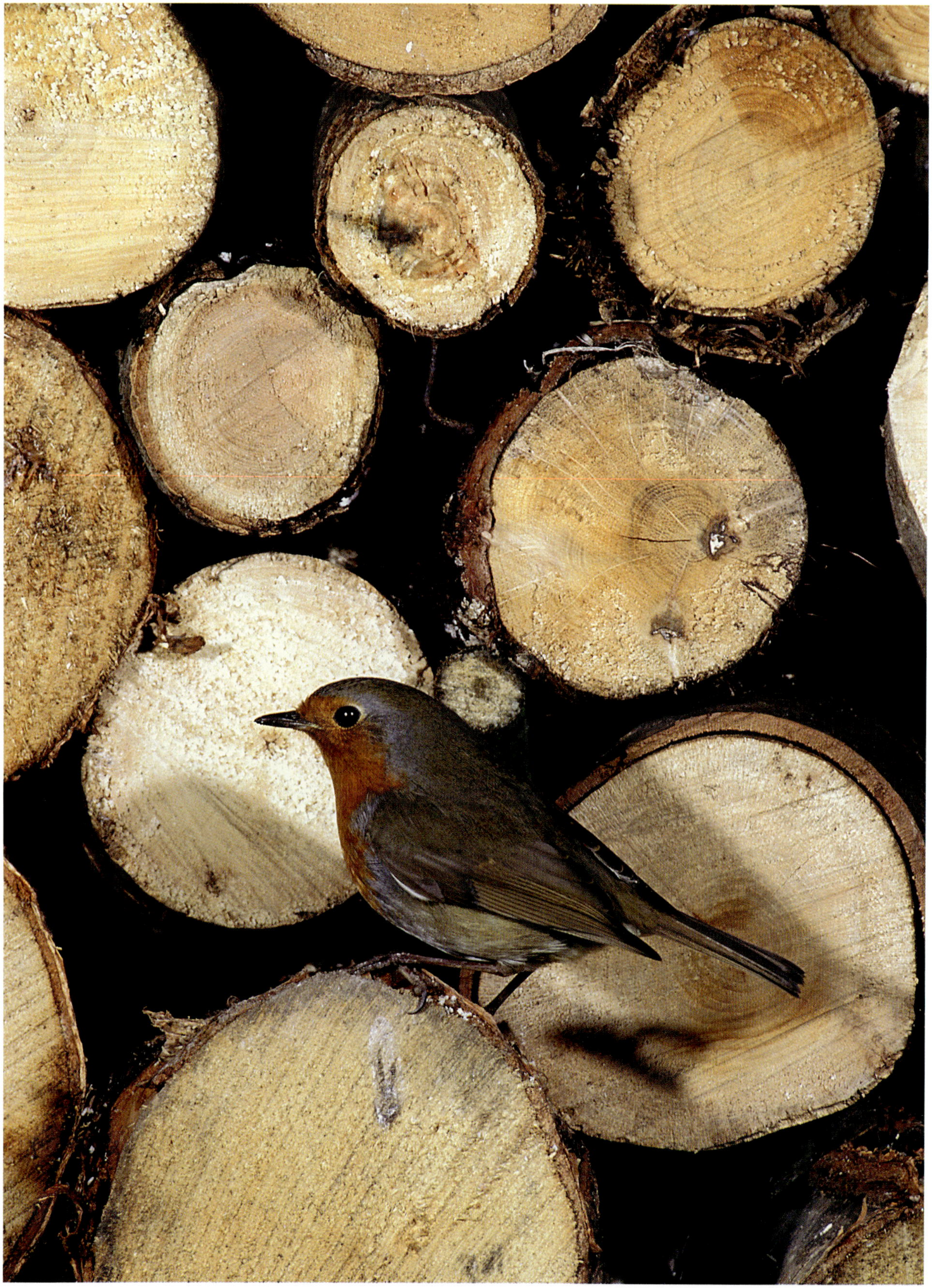

THIS SHOULD look like a robin sitting on a perfectly ordinary pile of logs. But there is a measure of skulduggery involved. The thick log, that provides the robin's perch, sticks out much further than the others. The log has been hollowed out with a sharp chisel and then filled with a tasty mixture of bacon fat and crushed peanuts. The camera is carefully placed so that it can't see the relative length of the log or its contents. But the robin quickly noticed both and soon came down for breakfast.

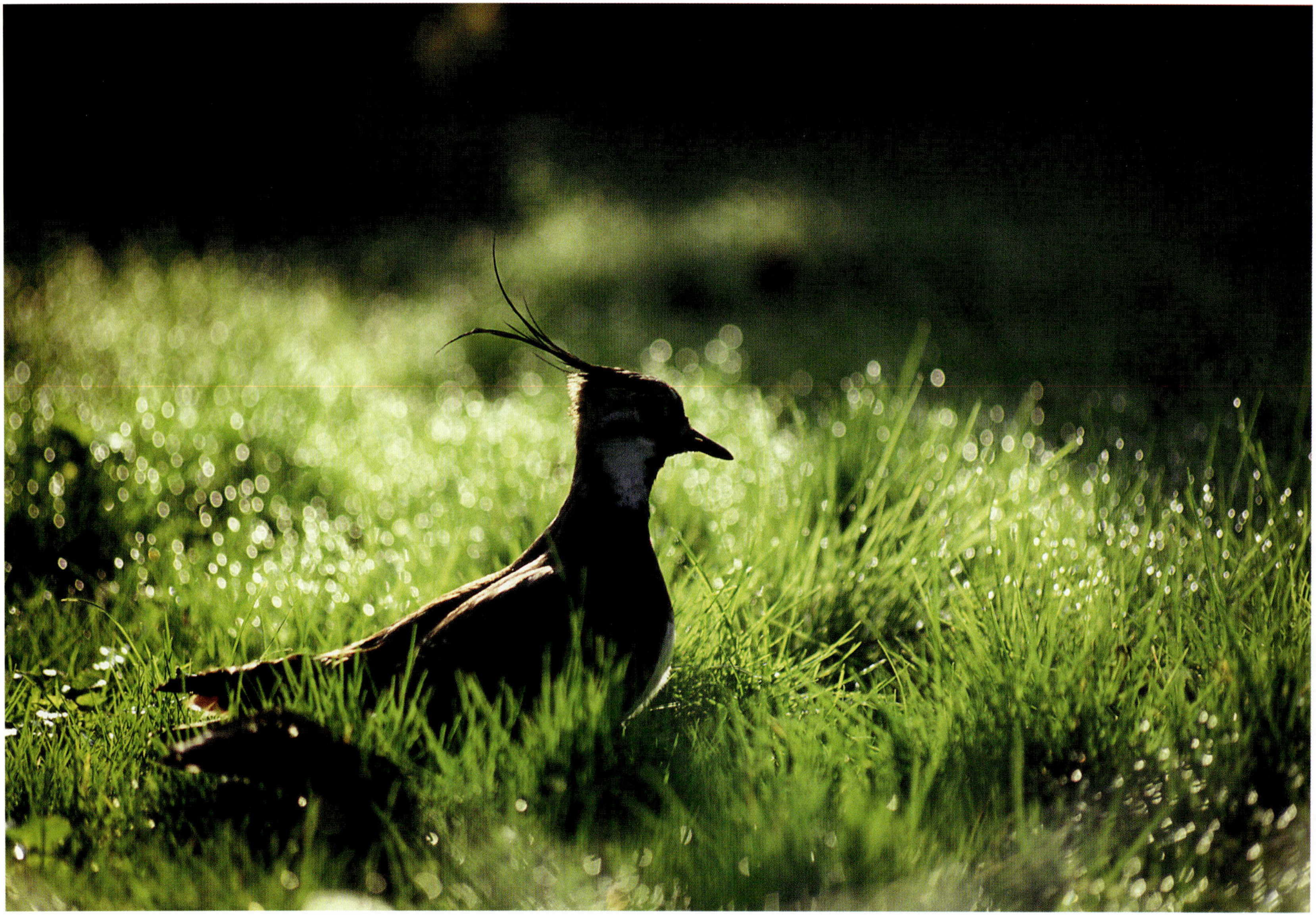

There's one unavoidable fact of life in wildlife photography. You have to get up early. The two hours following dawn is probably the best time to take pictures.

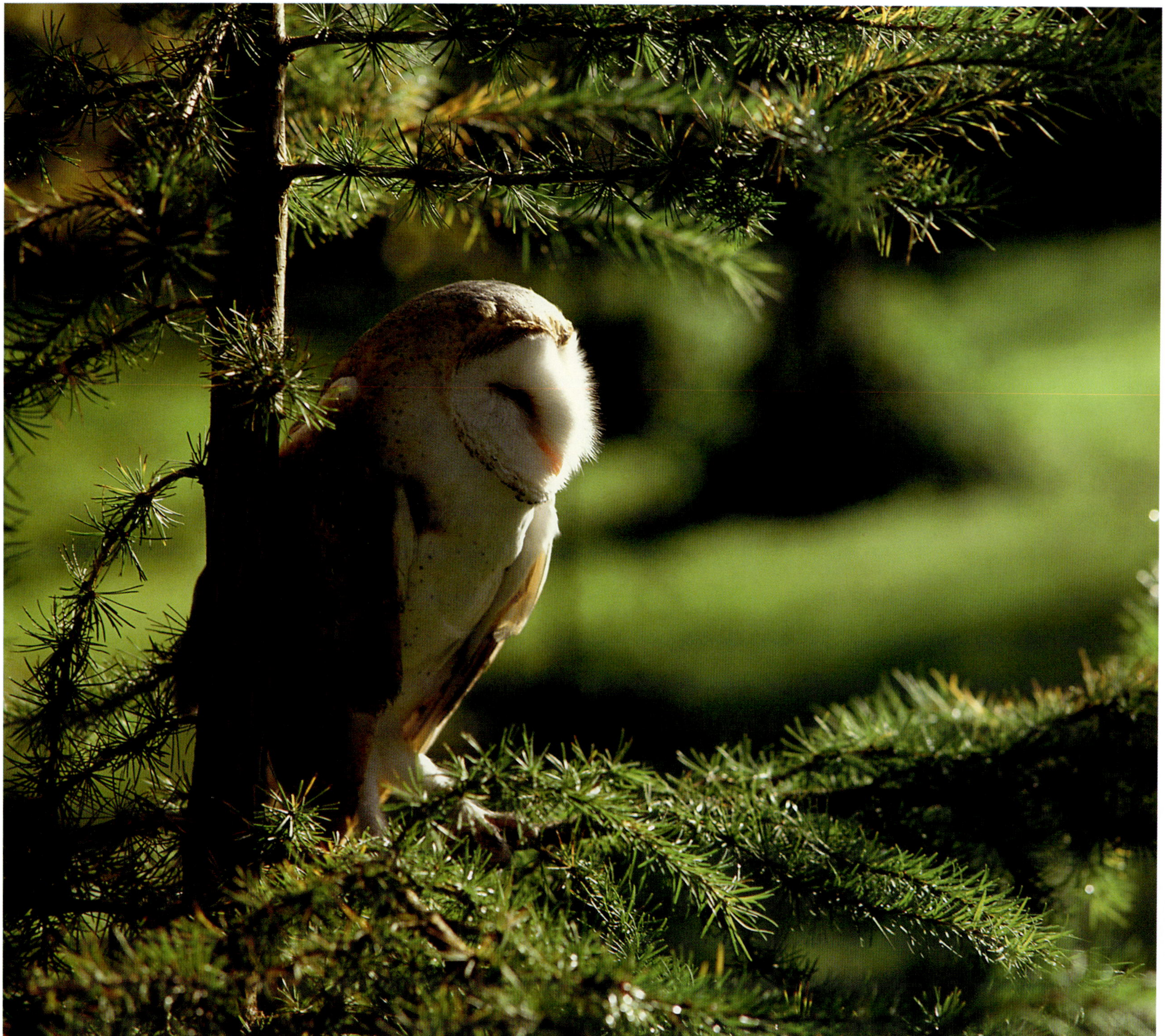

The word photography means 'drawing with light'. It's easy to forget that the quality of light itself can sometimes be the most important element of a picture. As the artist Caravaggio discovered in the seventeenth century, the subject can sometimes be completely irrelevant if the lighting is right.

This photograph was taken just after dawn, while the sun was still sitting on the eastern horizon. Taken any later, this picture would never have worked. Both the larch tree and the barn owl are simply props in this photograph. They contribute to the finished result but the low and intense sunlight is the real star.

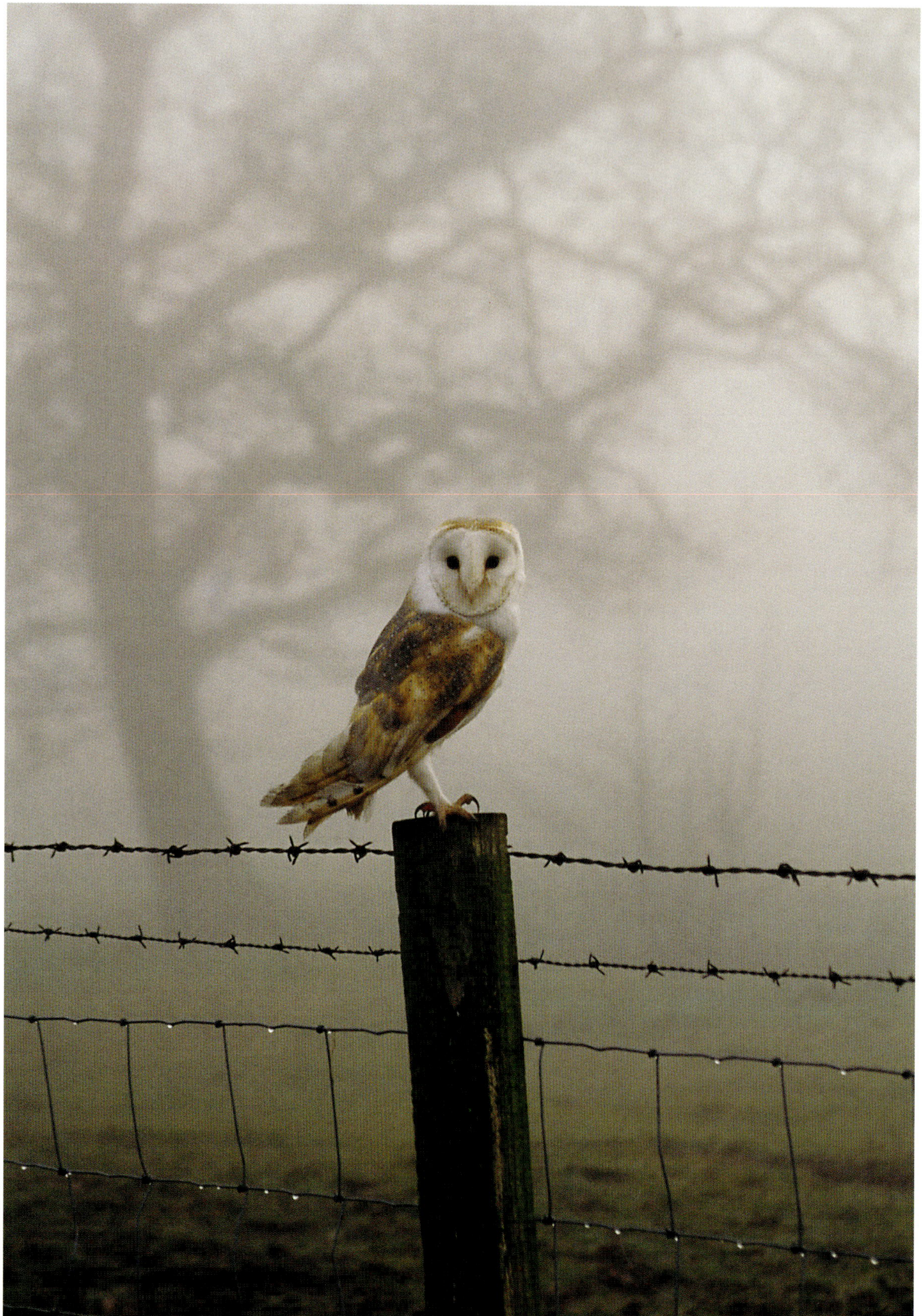

There are more than 1000 barn owl photographs in my collection and this is, by far, my favourite. Photography, like art and music, is highly subjective. There are no rights or wrongs. Technical experts can waffle on about resolution, depth of field and colour saturation but ultimately these are just peripheral details that cloud the real issue. It's much simpler than that – a picture either appeals to you or it doesn't. In the end a photograph is successful only if someone looks at it and likes what they see.

Wildlife photography is not just a matter of showing what an animal looks like. Sometimes it needs to go further than merely recording biological information. An evocative photograph can explain exactly how it felt to stand on that spot at the moment the picture was taken. Good pictures make you feel the sun on your face or the sand between your toes. Or, here, the cold damp air forming tiny droplets on your hair and eyelashes.

It takes only a moment's thought to realise that this is not a portrait of a barn owl. This is a picture of dawn and, within the landscape, there is also an owl. The bird takes up less than eight per cent of the frame. More important elements are the looming filigree outline of the tree in the background mist and the heavy, fat dewdrops clinging to the wire fence. This photograph was never meant to show what a barn owl looks like, because most people already know. It was taken to communicate a sense of place, to explain how it feels to stand in a field at dawn, to convey the cold dampness of a January morning and to show an insight into the way a barn owl lives.

Barn owls are crepuscular animals. This means that they are active at twilight. Under ideal conditions barn owls hunt for food around dusk and dawn. They sleep during the darkest hours of night and the brightest time of day.

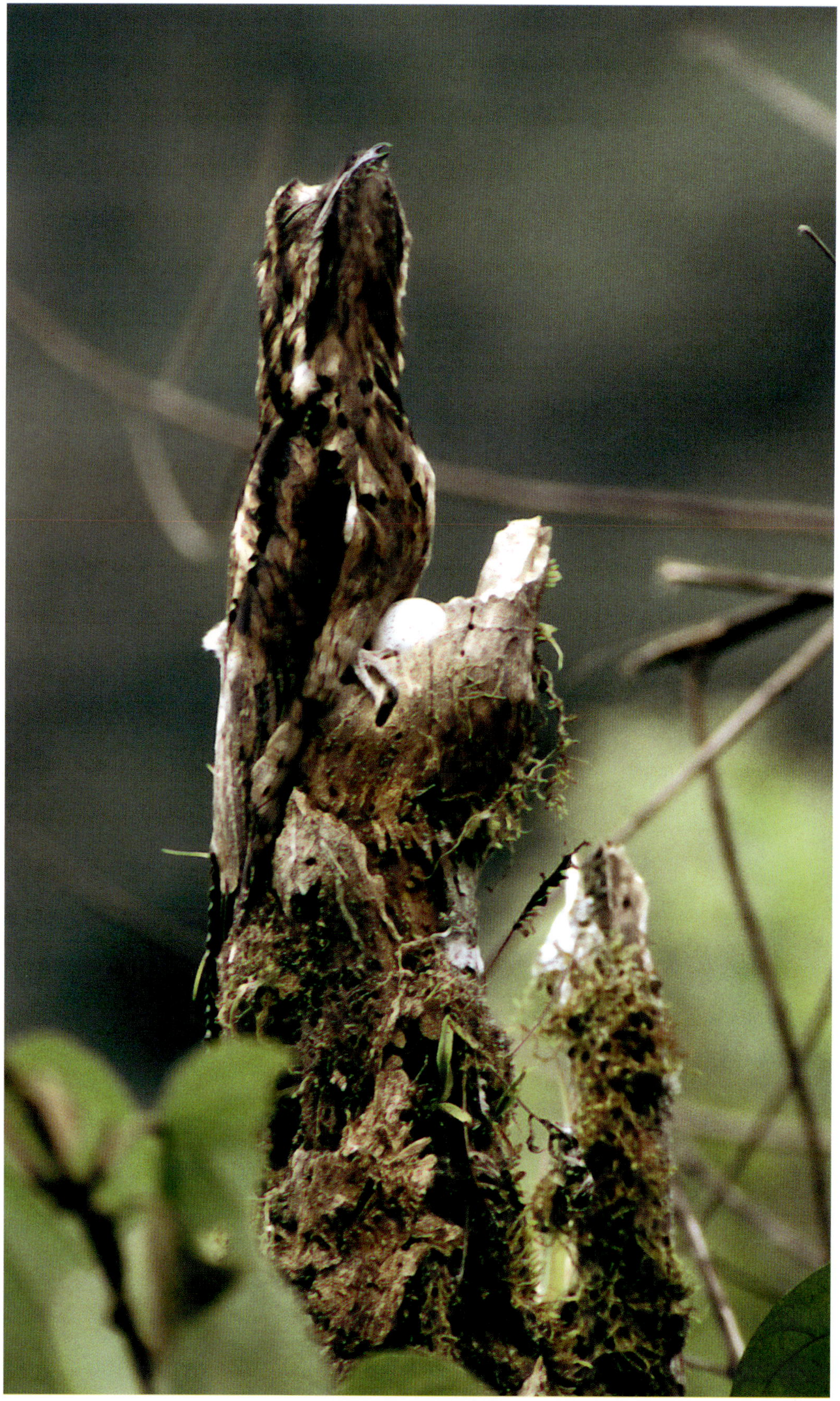

Technically perfect, close-up identification pictures can be a mistake with some species, because there are many different ways of portraying reality. The potoo is a large, insect-eating member of the owl family that lives in the tropical rainforests of South and Central America. They are shy, nocturnal creatures that studiously keep away from humans. The potoo's naturally demure behaviour alone is enough to make life difficult for anyone wishing to find one of these birds. But, on top of this, potoos have evolved an astonishing cryptic camouflage that effectively makes them completely invisible against the forest background.

This female is incubating her single egg, laid in a cup-shaped hole in the top of an old tree stump. Whenever a predator appears, in this case me, she tilts back her head, closes her eyes and stops breathing. The transformation is exquisite. In the blink of an eye the bird turns into a rotting branch, indistinguishable from the ranks of trees around. When trying to understand the potoo, this elegant subterfuge strategy is far more interesting than its physical appearance.

Common Potoo,
Amazon Rainforest

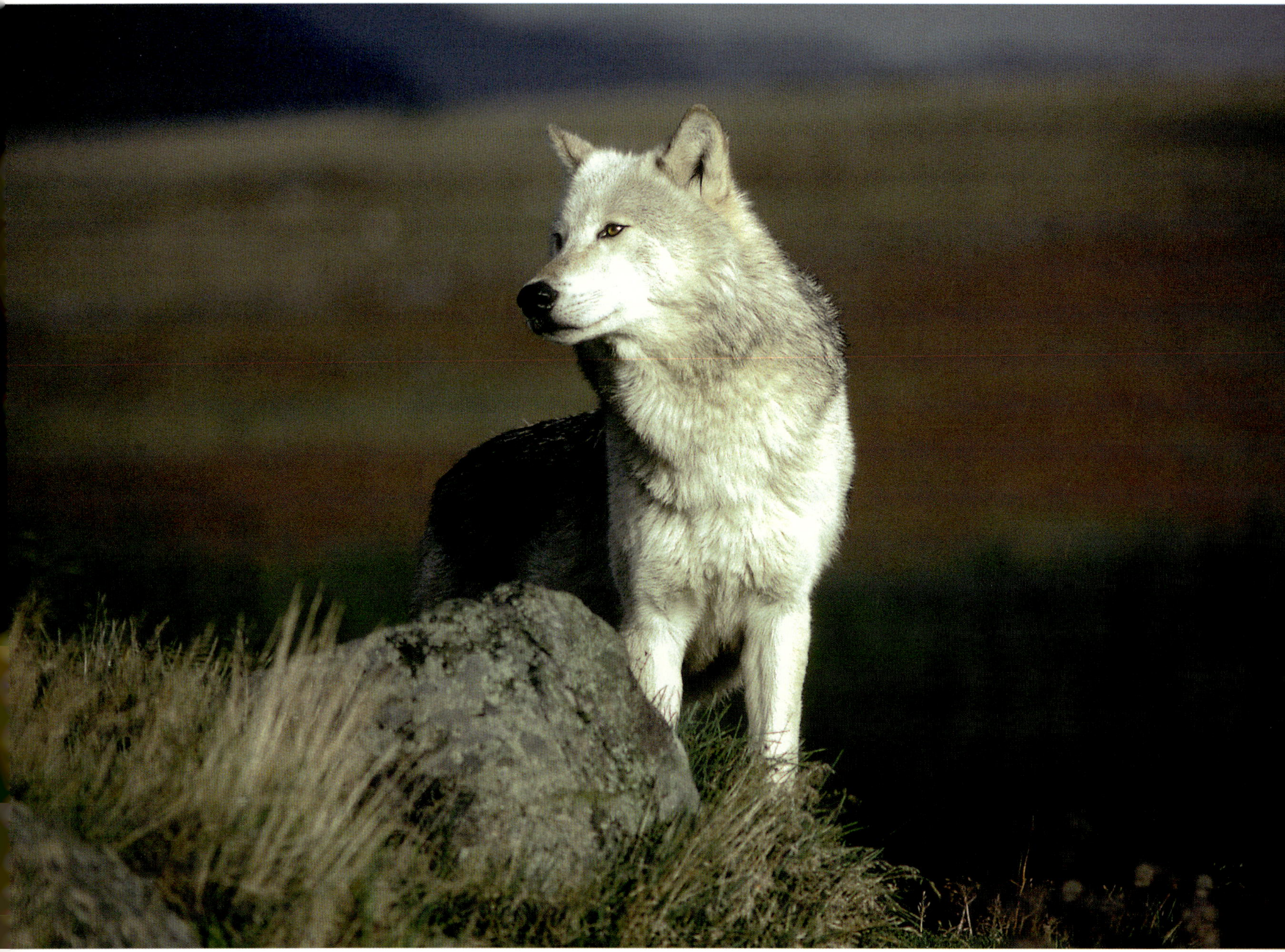

THIS PICTURE is in for a purely selfish reason. I could not possibly produce a book of wildlife photographs without including a portrait of a timber wolf.

For me they are one of the world's most fascinating and misunderstood animals.

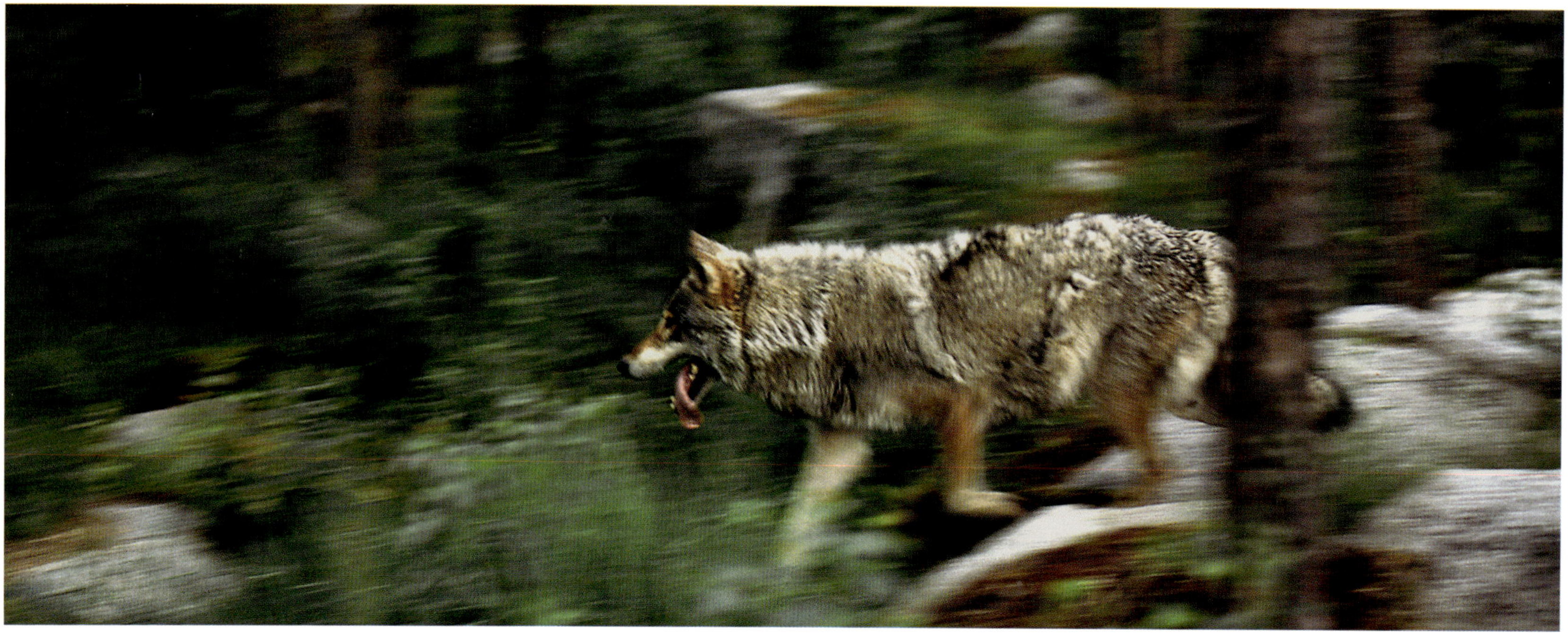

The photograph on the previous page is a conventional shot of a timber wolf. It is sharp and well exposed, but this is just one of the many possible techniques that can be used to capture an animal on film.

The picture on the left is far less formal. While the previous picture shows what a wolf looks like, this is meant to show what it's like to see a wolf. The two are not at all the same. A wolf running through a wood is quiet, silent and anxious not to be seen, particularly when there are humans anywhere near. Even the most distant view is incredibly fortunate. The most you can hope for is a quick glimpse as the wolf disappears through the trees.

This picture is meant to convey something of that vanishing moment.

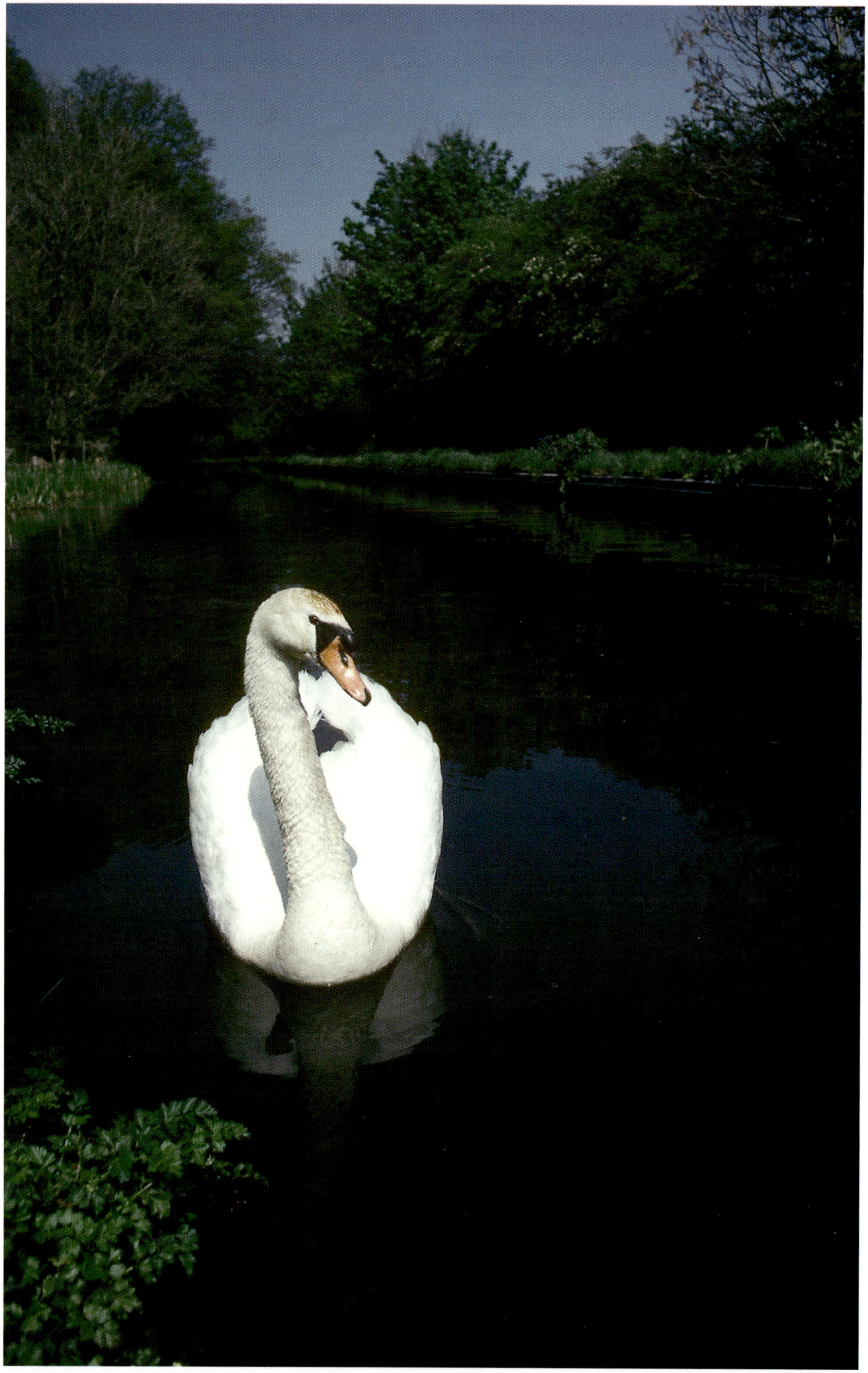

A LONG TIME AGO a venerable expert from a by-gone age announced that swans were not really suitable subjects for serious wildlife photographers, because they were just not wild enough. I remember thinking then that he was wrong, and that conviction has grown stronger. People often become too hooked on the exotic, dangerous and rare species. It's as if those random anthropomorphic qualities make some animals more important or worthwhile than any others. My job isn't to judge the relative merits of each species; no one should have to carry out that impossible task.

If mute swans were rare, people would cross continents for the chance to look at them. Swans are graceful, stunningly beautiful creatures that are just as worthy of our respect and admiration as any other animal on the planet. Even after twenty-five years I still think they make wonderful photographic subjects.

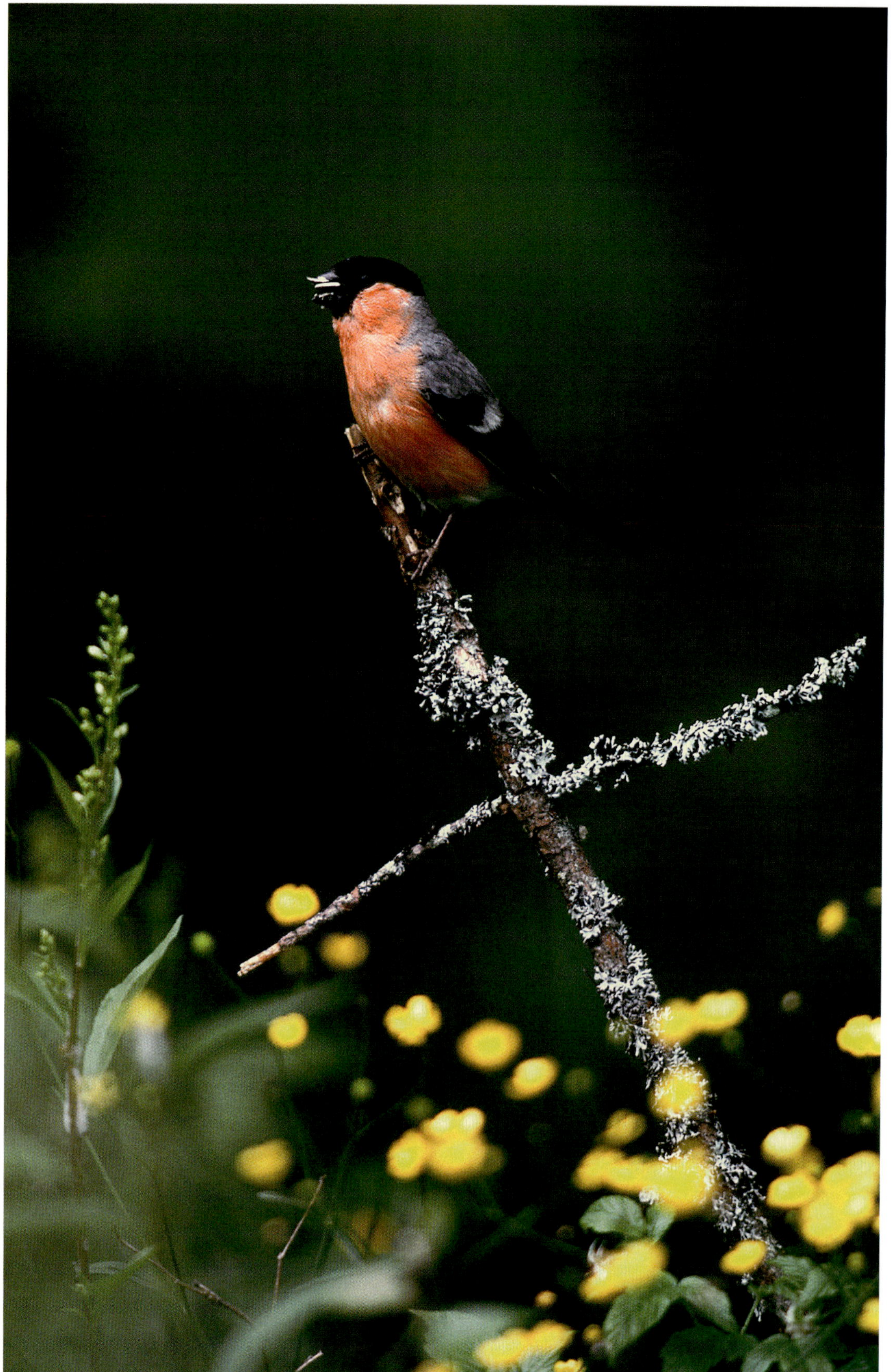

When the sun is out and I'm in an unfamiliar place with a few hours to kill, I sometimes find an attractive corner, scatter some food around and sit with a camera to see if anything turns up. I would be too embarrassed to describe this as work, as there are far worse ways of spending an afternoon. But, in truth, these lazy days are usually well worthwhile.

This male bullfinch was photographed in a woodland clearing that was new to me. The most attractive part of the scene was a clump of buttercups growing in the centre, where the sun's rays were not shaded by the trees. A quick search in the forest revealed a lovely cruciform twig that was encrusted with lichen and made a perfect photogenic perch. I hid a handful of nuts on the ground between the flowers and pushed the perch carefully into the soil just behind.

It took a while before anything arrived. So I was forced to sit in the warm afternoon sun, listening to the soft sounds of the woodland and thinking that my job is sometimes quite tolerable. On its first visit the bullfinch was spooky and quickly disappeared having quickly snatched some food. But it soon relaxed and I ran through a whole roll of film. Some days it's just good to be alive.

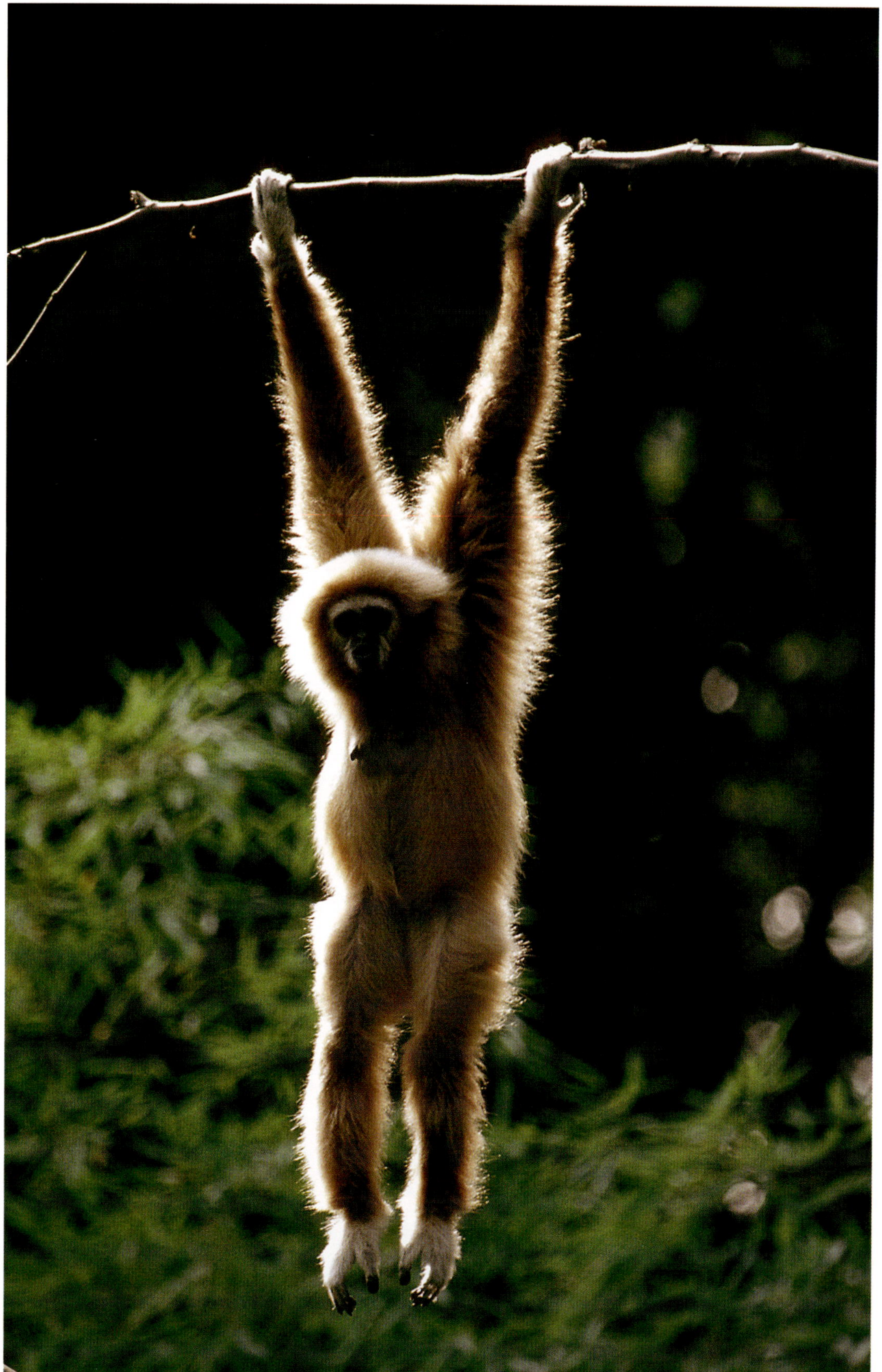

WHEN the animal appears in the right light, all I have to do is press the button and enjoy the experience.

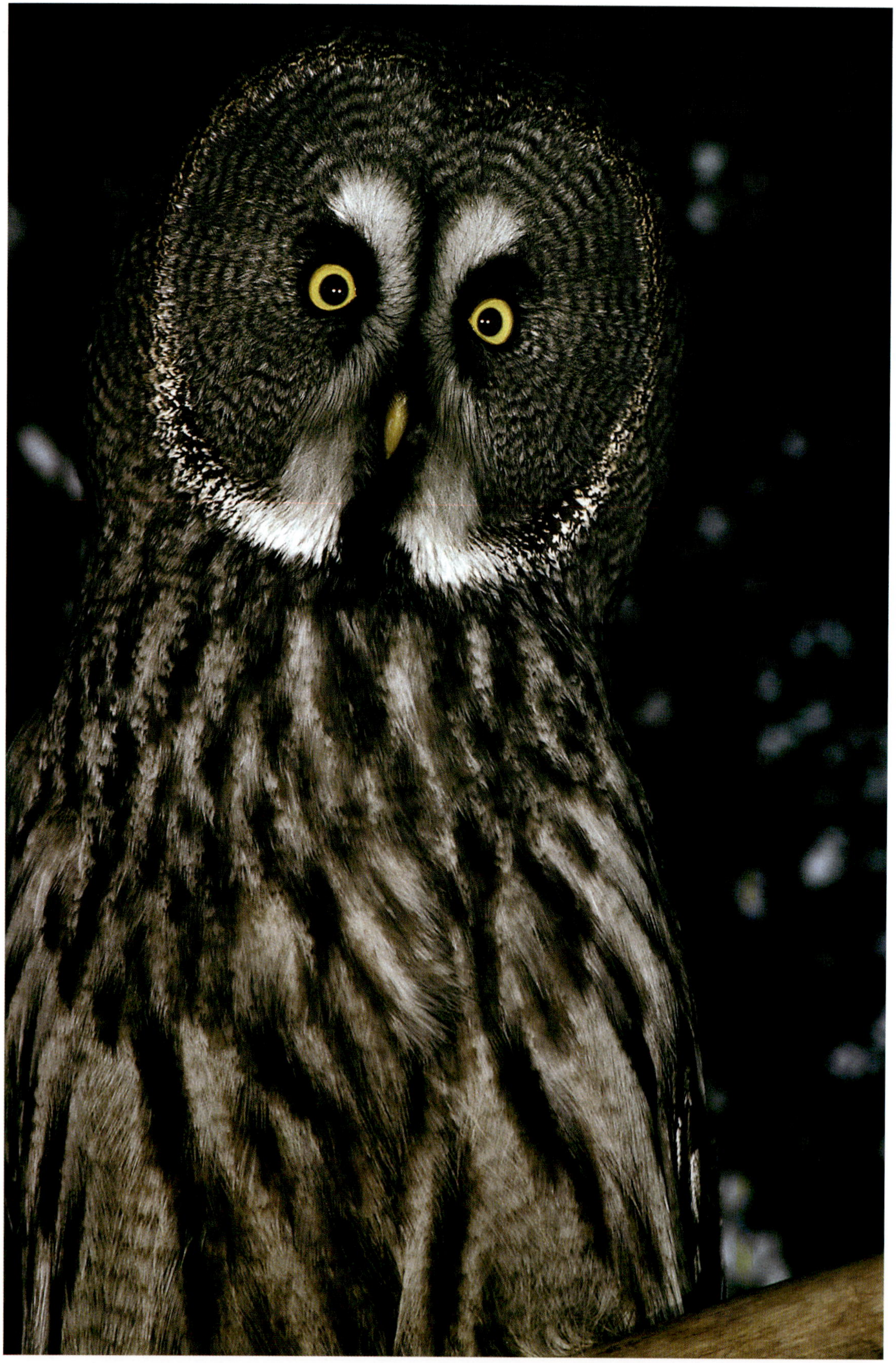

Great grey owls are creatures of the far north. They live in Scandinavia, Russia and Canada, where winter lasts for six months and the temperature can drop to minus forty degrees.

I find great grey owls irresistible because of the perpetual look of surprise they wear.

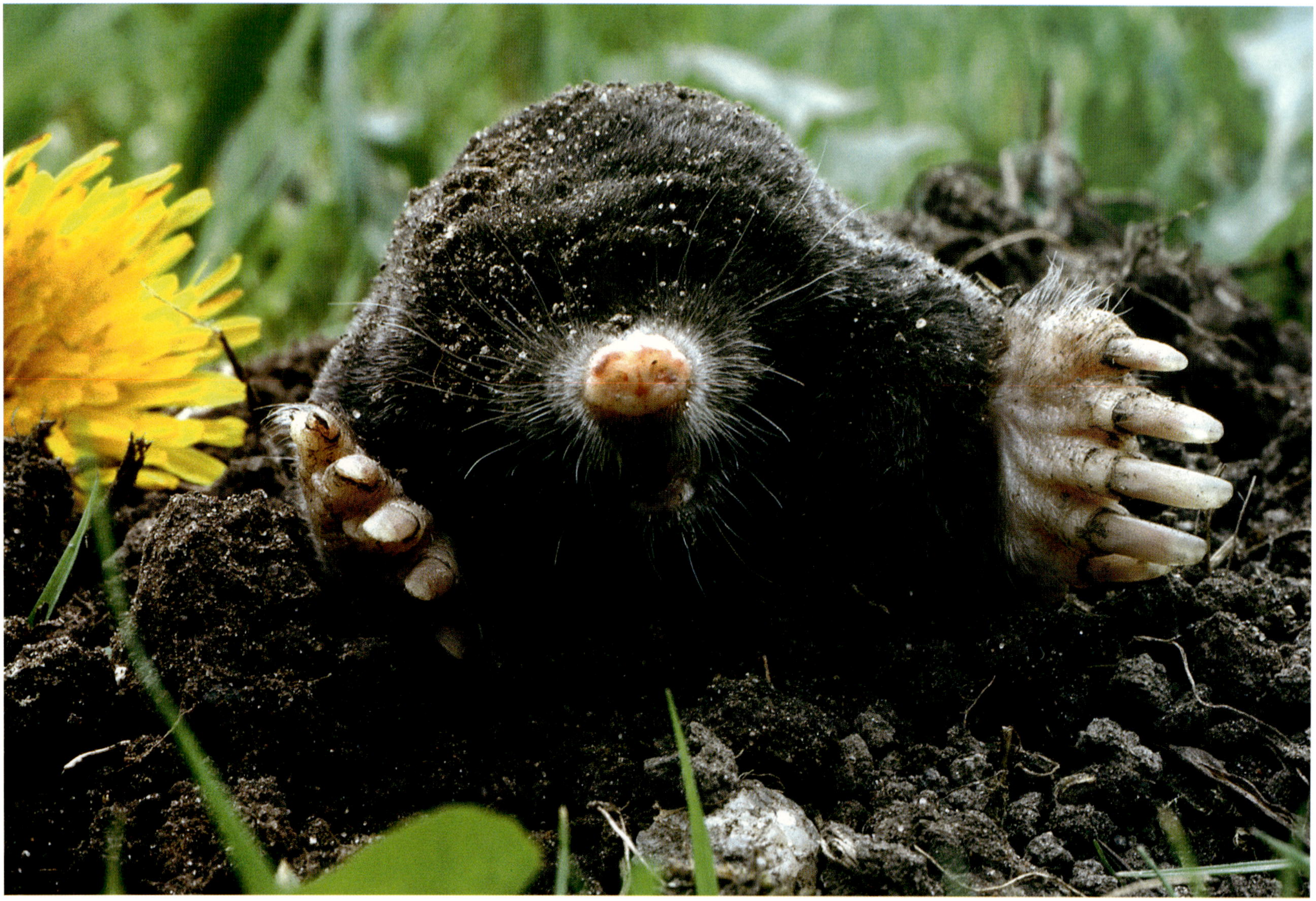

MOLES are one of our most numerous and widespread mammals, but few people ever see them. We only know of their existence by the tell-tale mounds of fresh earth scattered around our prize lawns. These are the waste heaps of the underground tunnel system that allows moles to patrol their territory and find food in safety. Above ground they are at risk from foxes, owls, stoats, cats and an assortment of other predators that see moles as an ideal snack.

Wildlife photographers should not only concentrate on exotic animals that are outside our experience. It's just as important to take a close look at everyday species, especially if those creatures are elusive and rarely seen.

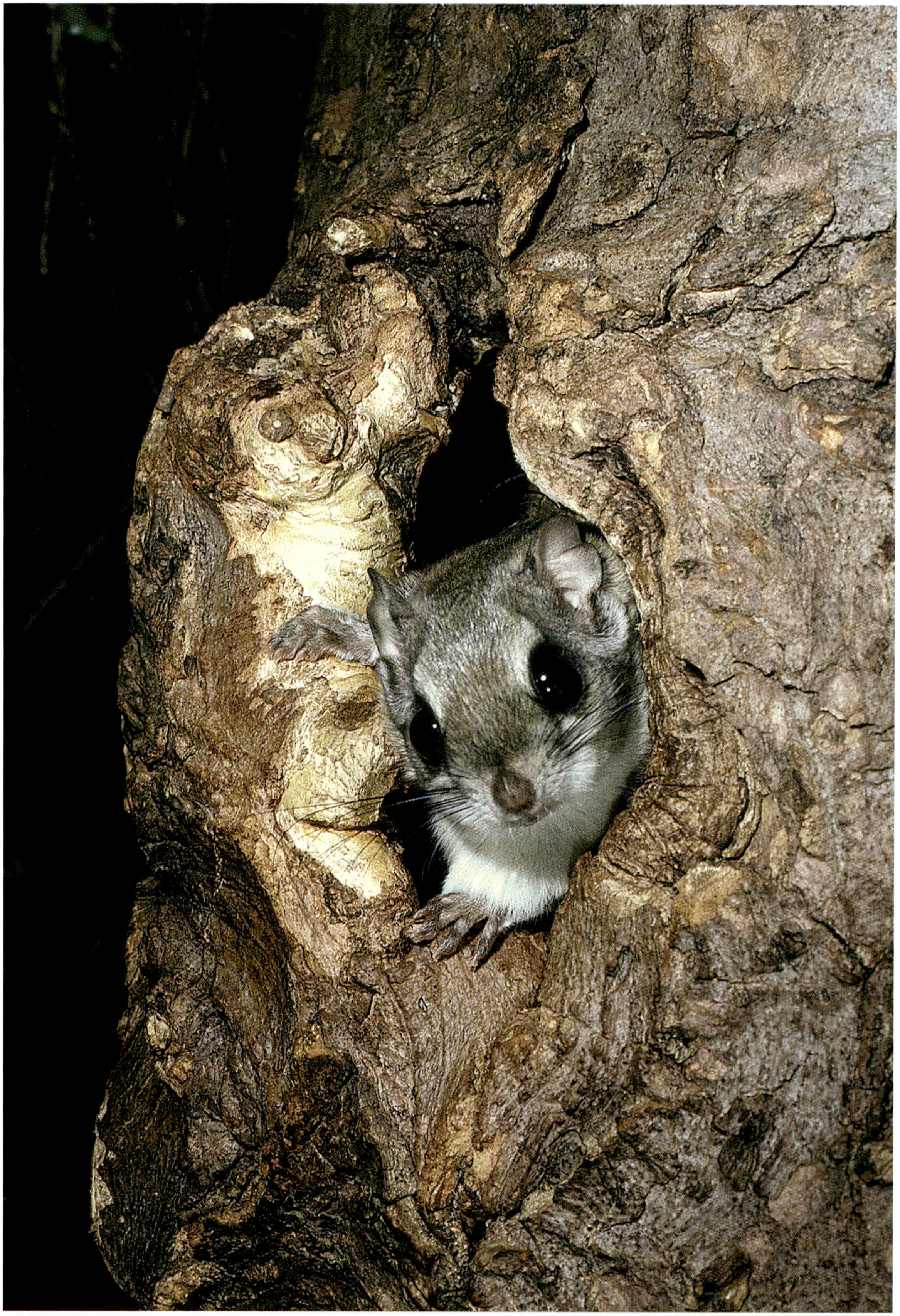

PROFESSIONALLY there are a handful of universal rules that should be borne in mind when trying to produce a successful wildlife photograph. Early morning light is better than mid-day light, dew drops always look good, baby animals make pictures much more saleable, blue skies are more appealing than cloudy skies, animals making eye contact with the camera always produce more striking portraits.

And small cuddly creatures peeping out from holes are absolutely irresisitible.

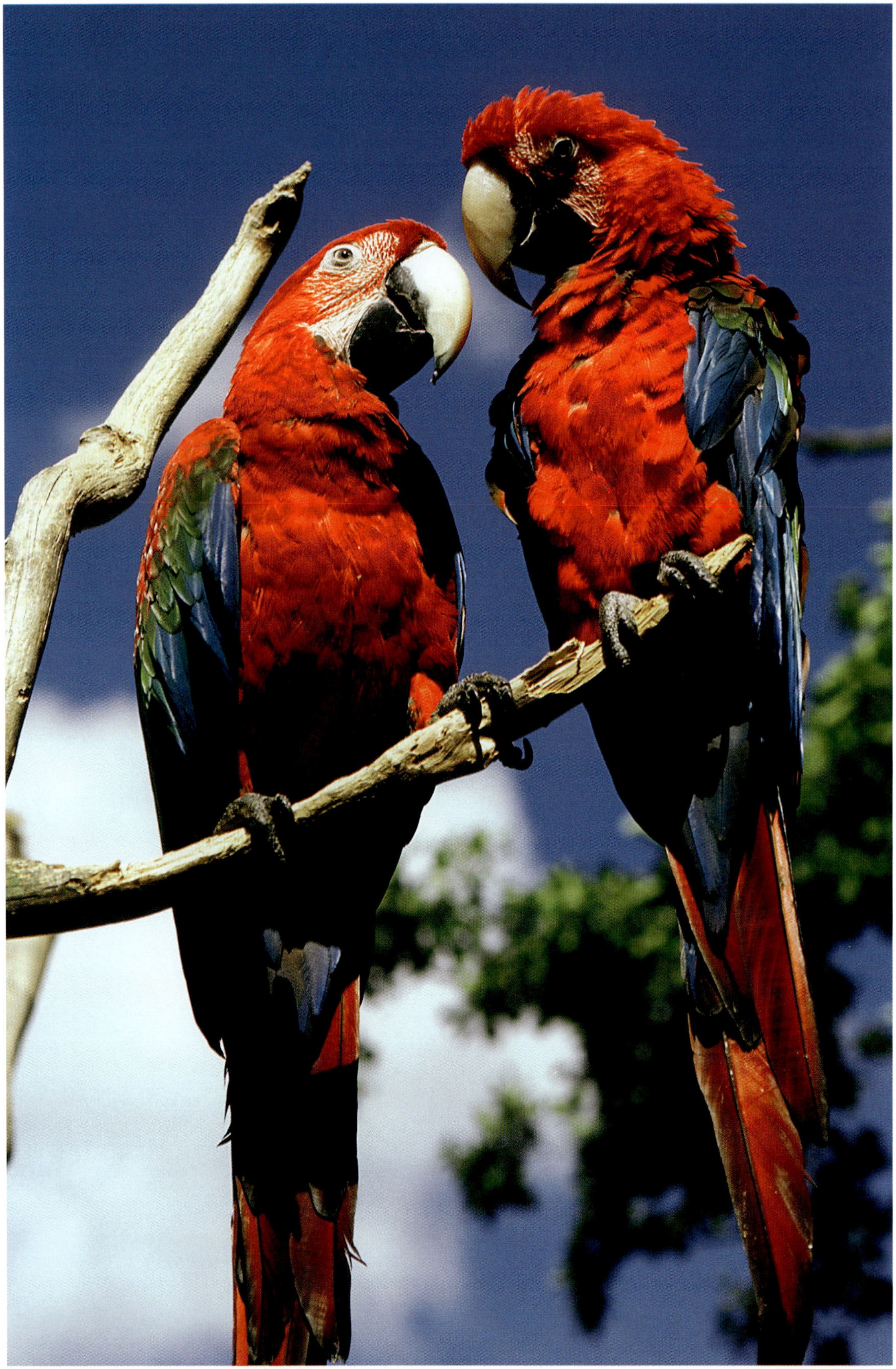

THE COLOUR of the sky can make or break a picture. A vivid blue is truly spectacular, particularly when set against the glorious plumage of these scarlet macaws.

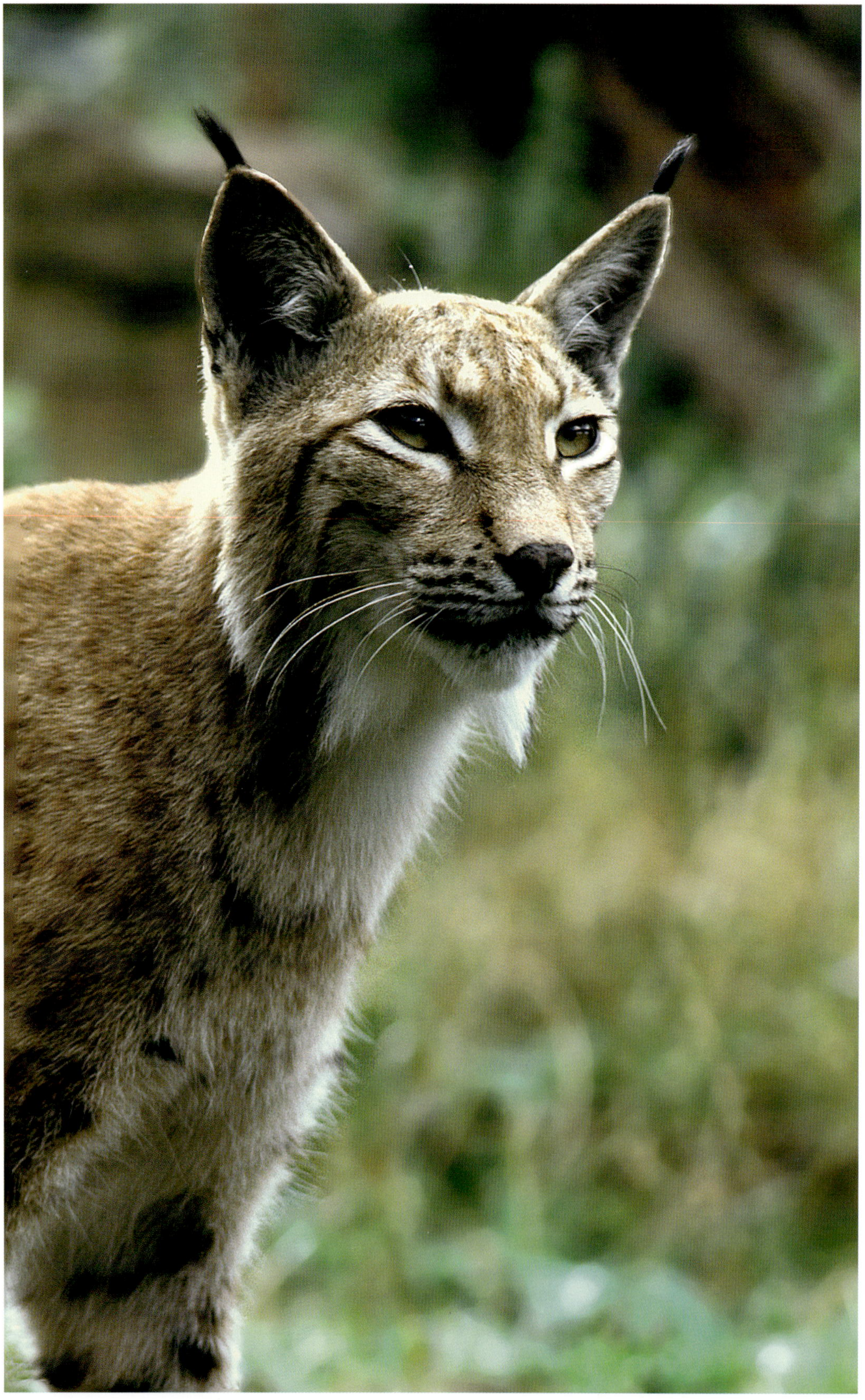

The northern lynx lives in Europe and North America. Although the population in Canada is healthy, everywhere else the animal is in trouble. A thousand years ago the lynx was found all over Europe, including Britain. They are now confined to a tiny number of wilderness areas in Scandinavia and eastern Europe.

A lynx is about the size of a medium pet dog; it is a long-legged animal that moves with unusually silent grace, even for a cat. It is a solitary creature that comes out mainly at night, although, like most other members of the family, the lynx has a passion for sunbathing.

The modern name lynx comes originally from the ancient Greek word *lunx* meaning light coloured and bright-eyed.

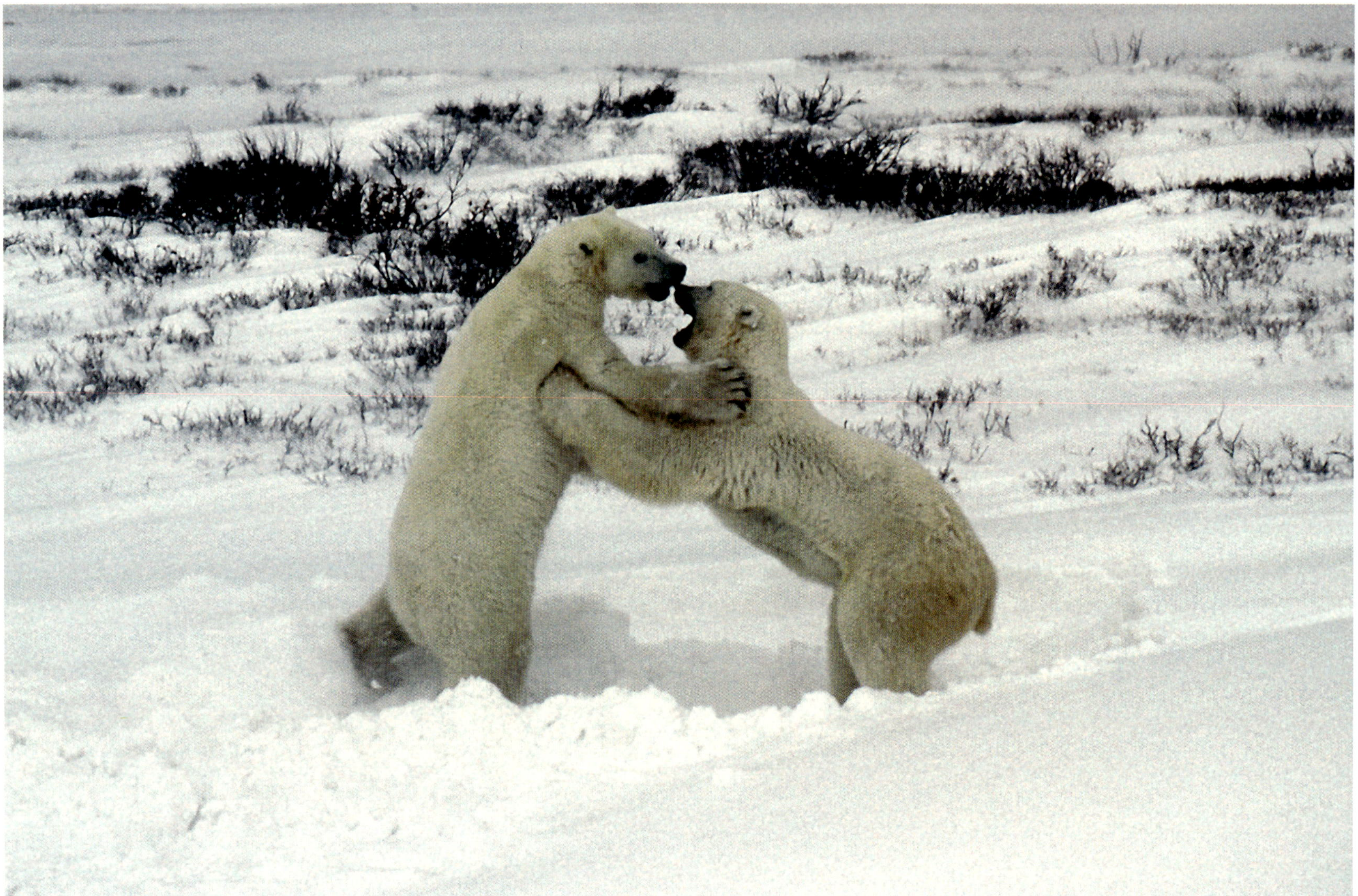

Polar bears are creatures of the arctic; they only live in the frozen landscape of the Northern Hemisphere. The Inuit people of the far north have their own word for these animals – it translates as ice-bear. This is a perfect name for an animal that does not like open water or dry land.

Polar bears like the frozen sea, where they can wander far and wide searching for food. Seals form the biggest part of a polar bear's diet. Seals are fish-eaters that spend their days feeding in the Arctic Ocean. They are skilled divers but, being mammals, they must come up regularly to breathe. When the sea is frozen each seal has breathing holes in the ice, kept open by constantly nibbling fresh ice as it forms. Hungry polar bears wait by these holes until a seal appears. Then with a single thump of a massive front foot, the bear breaks the seal's neck and drags it out of the water.

This works well for nine months of the year, but even the arctic has a summer. For three months of the year the sea-ice breaks up and the bears are forced onto land, where there is little to eat. Their bodyweight drops and they lose condition. They are forced to wait until the temperature drops and the pack ice re-appears. When the first snow falls and ice crystals start to form the bears instinctively know that they will soon be able to hunt again. But it will be a while before the sea-ice is strong enough to support a polar bear's vast weight. A fully-grown male weighs about the same as a small car. The bears are hungry and raring to go. To pass the time and prepare their muscles for the hunt the bears spend hours mock-fighting. They stand on their hind legs thumping each other with paws the size of shovels. They chase each other along the coast, biting and wrestling.

These battles are prolonged and dramatic but the animals don't get hurt. This is known as displacement activity. The bears desperately want to hunt; they can't, so they do something else instead. For the weeks between the first frost and the final freezing of the sea, the polar bears' mock fighting ritual is one of the great sights of the natural world.

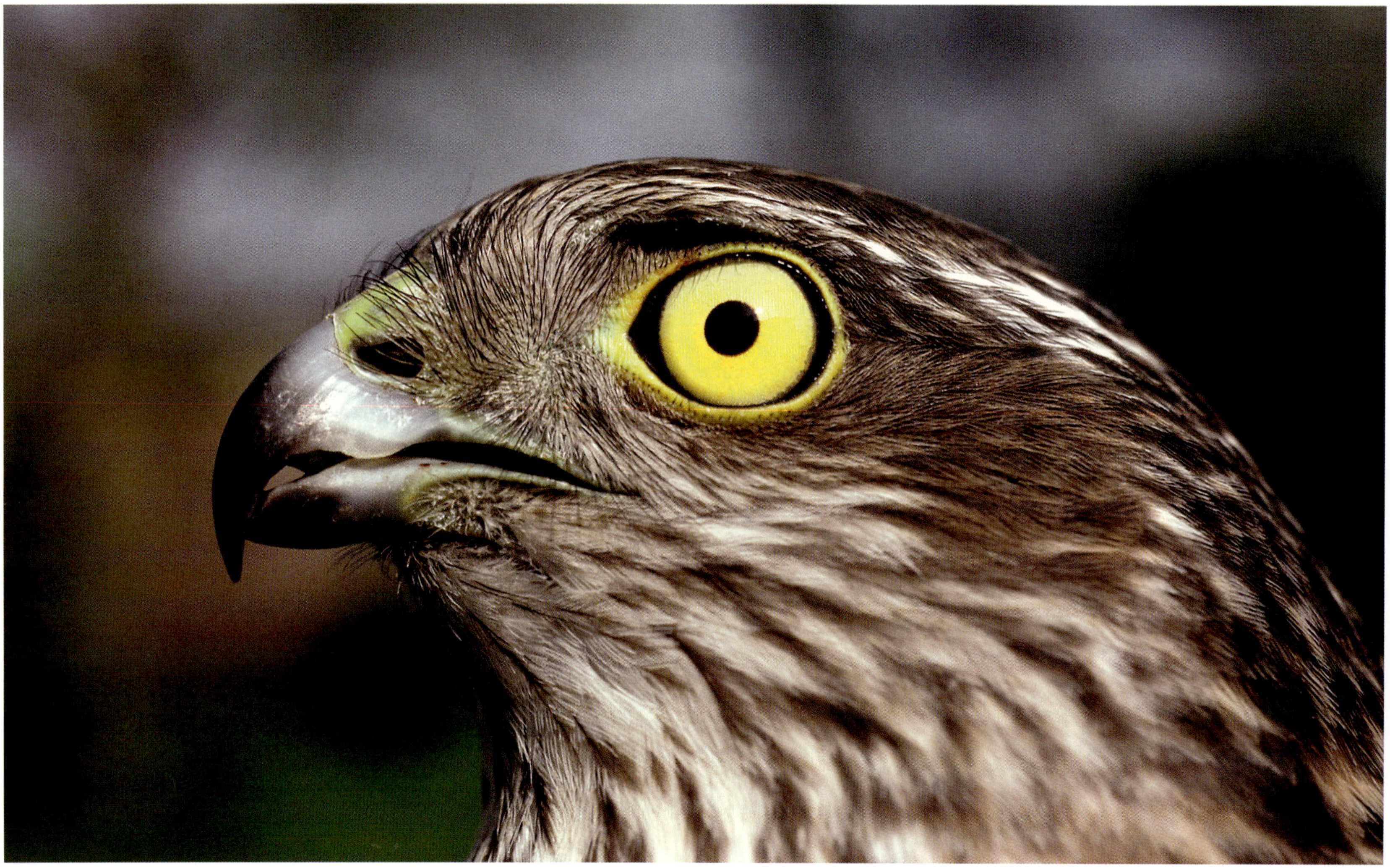

Close-up shots of a head are one of the classic portraits for wildlife photographers. Particularly when the head belongs to a predator like a sparrowhawk.

Images of hunting animals exert a powerful pull on humans, even if we are not aware of the effect. Publishers and photographers have known for years that predators' faces have a mesmeric effect on viewers. This knowledge is hugely important when working out what pictures to include in a book.

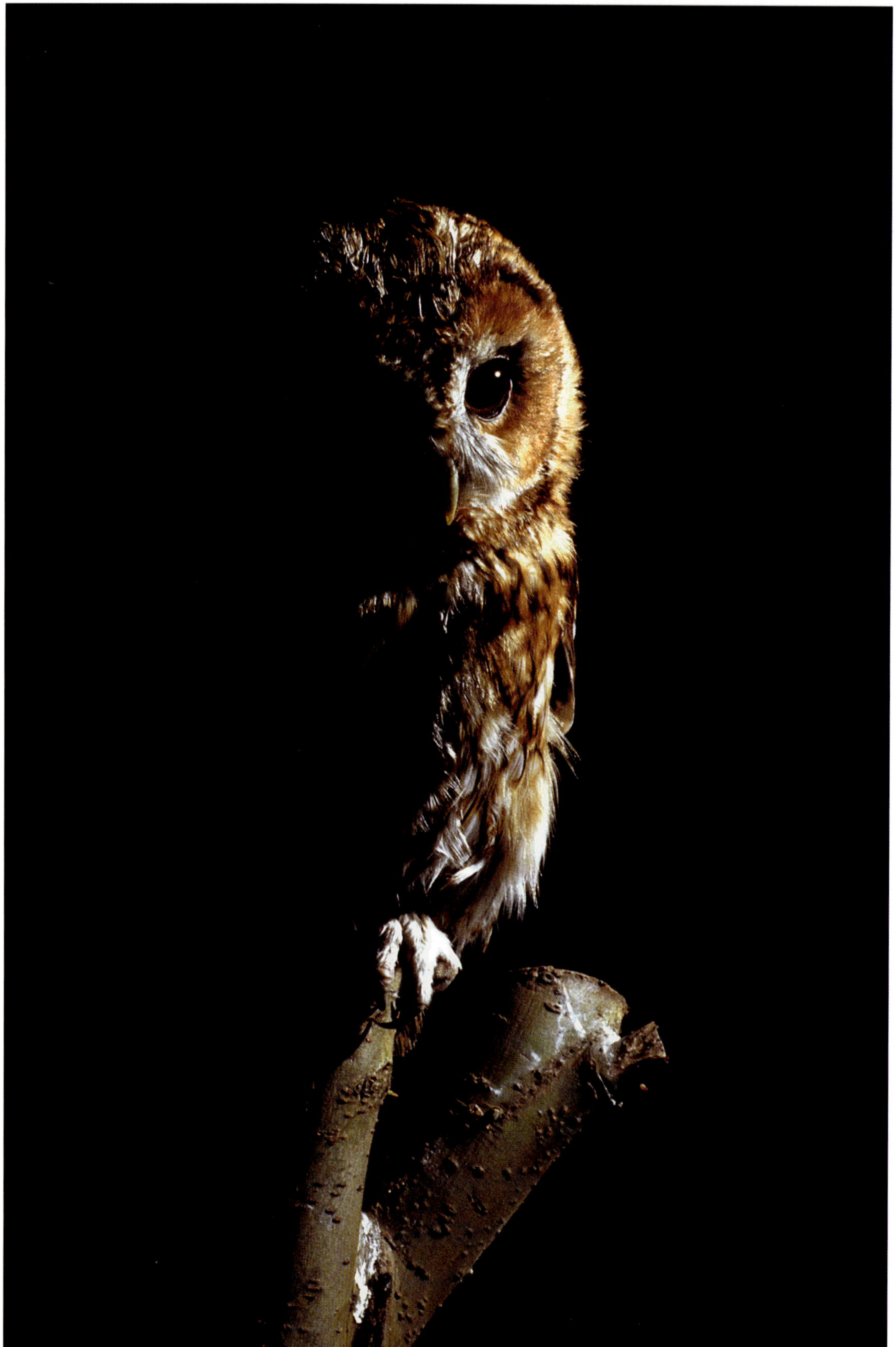

Tawny owls are very rarely seen, despite being the most common and widespread owl in the country. Tawnies prefer to hunt under the cloak of darkness; they spend their days dozing in quiet trees well away from all disturbance. Here they hide until the last of the sun's rays disappear, before venturing out to find food. Tawny owls only move during the day when disturbed by enemies, and at night their cryptic camouflage makes them all but invisible against the background gloom of a woodland canopy.

Barn owls are seen far more frequently than tawny owls, which is ironic as tawnies outnumber barn owls by perhaps three hundred to one. But the two species have very different colouring. The snow white underside of a barn owl flying against a jet black sky cannot be overlooked by even the most unobservant passer-by. But there are life-long wildlife enthusiasts who have completely failed to track down the almost supernaturally elusive tawny owl.

To show this enigmatic quality in a photograph, it was simply a matter of arranging the lighting carefully. A single flash from one side provided just the right mixture of detail and mystery to convey the owl's wraith-like nature.

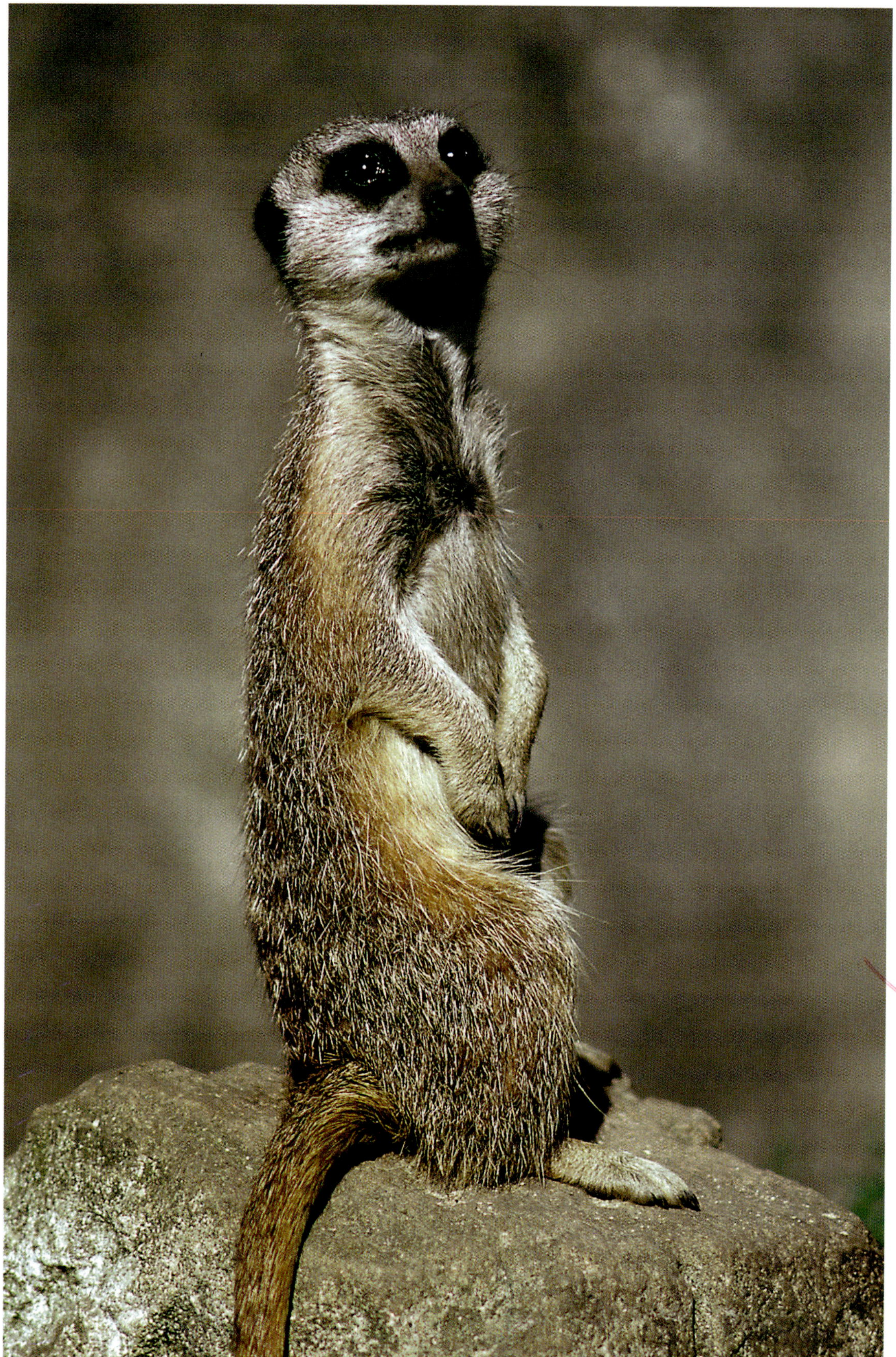

Apart from their lack of sheer physical power, small animals have a distinct disadvantage in the constant life and death struggle between prey and predators. It may be an obvious thing to say but their eyes are just too close to the floor. When danger threatens small animals need time to escape. This requires a good early warning system that detects enemies before they get too close. Low-slung eyes give very restricted vision of the surrounding landscape and greatly reduce the chances of survival.

The meerkats of southern Africa live in small troops that wander the plains in search of the insects, small mammals and fruit that make up their diet. But they themselves are hunted by larger predators such as jackals and eagles. The short-legged meerkats cannot easily see danger while feeding on all fours, so they redress the balance a little by sitting up on their hind legs to raise their eyes and get a wider view. But they can improve on this technique by scanning the countryside from the top of tall rocks or termite hills. The meerkats take turns to act as sentries; when something potentially unpleasant appears they chitter a loud, harsh warning call and the whole group runs for cover. It works beautifully.

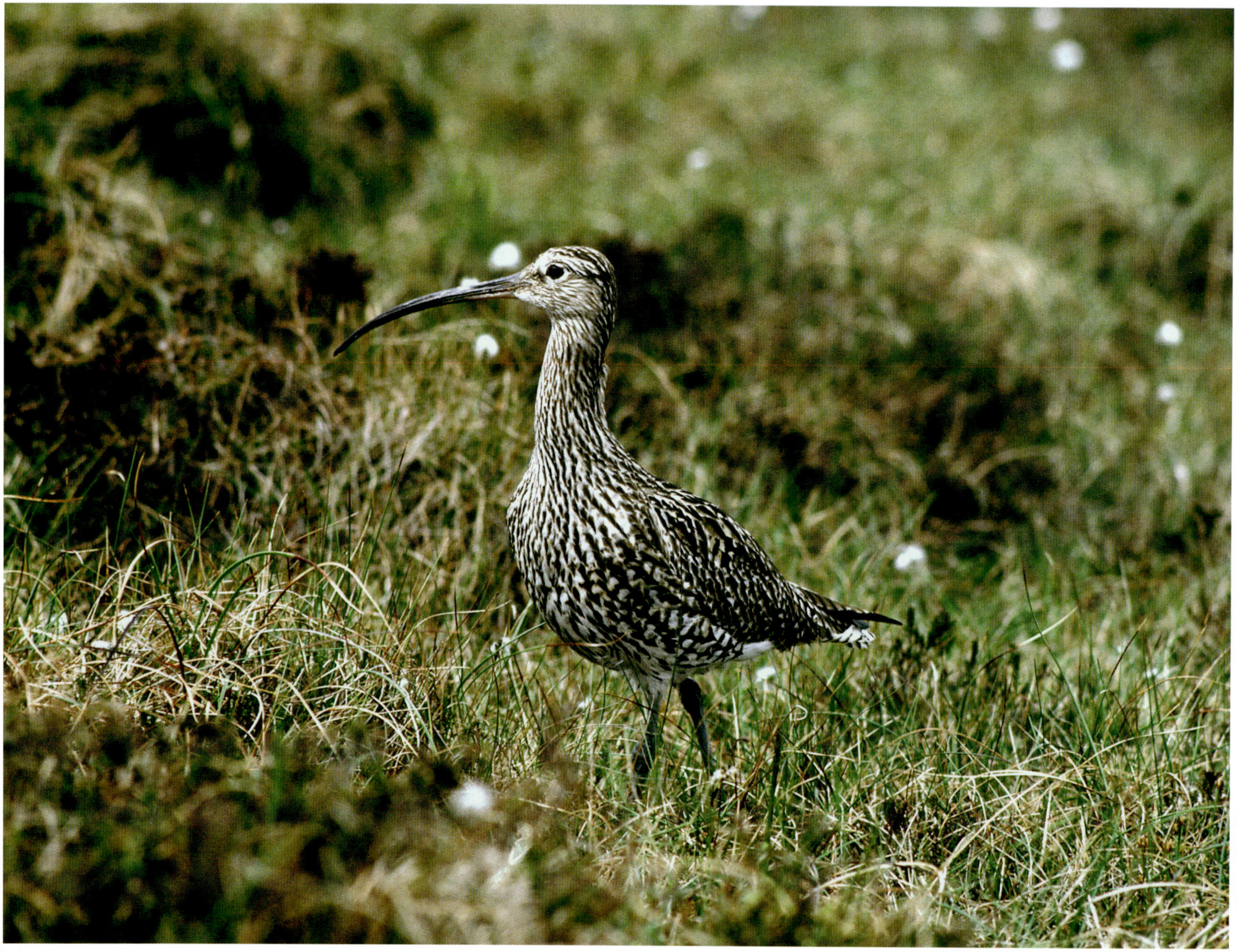

All jobs must have their high and low points; mine is no different. There are some places and animals that are more appealing or moving than others. For me this is a perfect example.

This curlew was photographed on remote moorland in the Hebrides. From where I sat, there was no sign of twenty-first century Man. The landscape wasn't scarred by roads or endless lines of telegraph poles, not a scrap of litter could be seen amongst the cotton grass and heather. To every horizon there was only wilderness. My ears weren't assaulted by the muffled drone of distant traffic that always seems to intrude on so many other beautiful spots.

The only sounds were the occasional trill of a hovering skylark and the haunting whistle of a curlew. Surely one of the most evocative sounds of the British countryside.

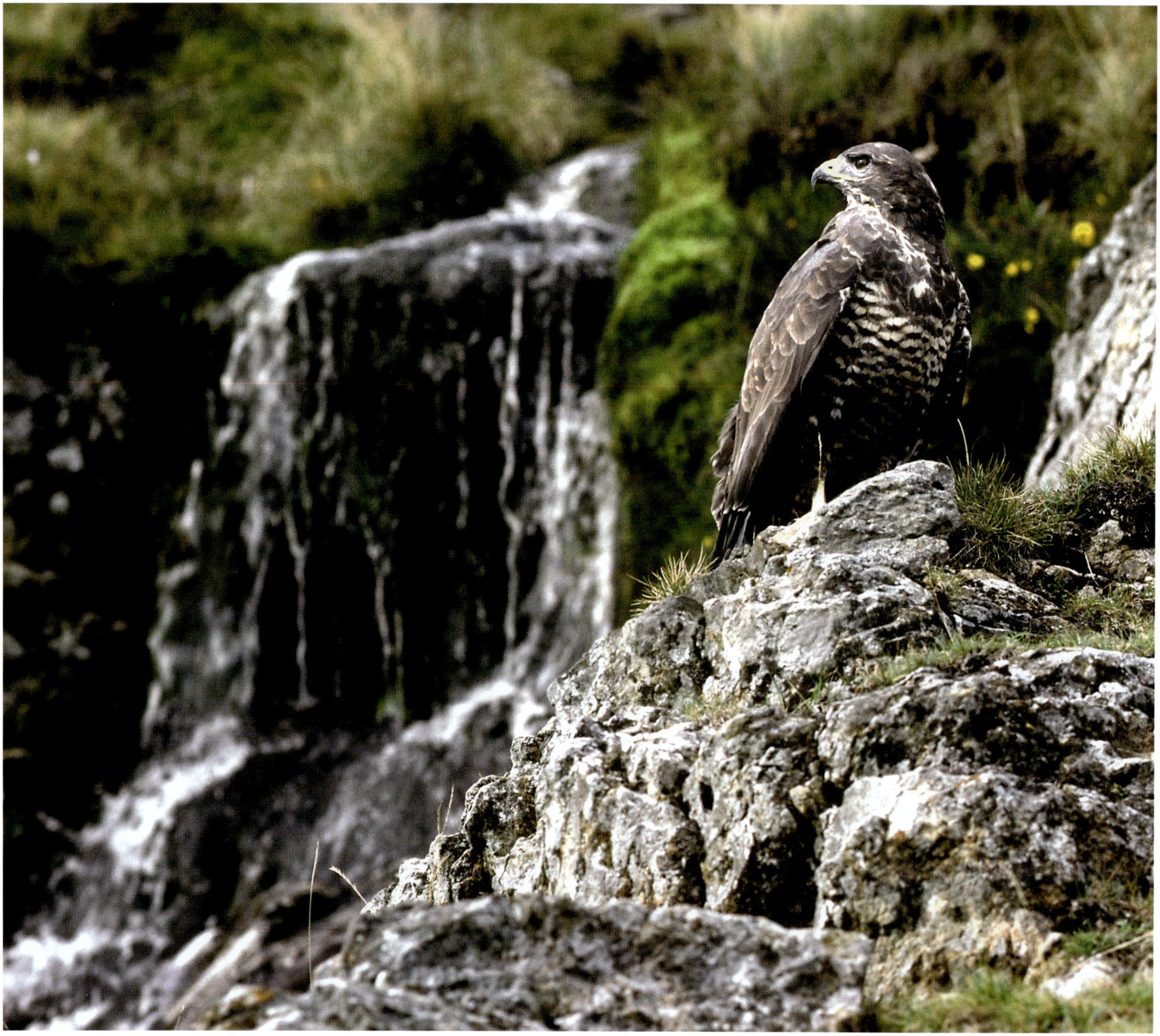

When dealing with a new species, I always try to work out how to encapsulate as much as possible into one single shot. Is there a way of showing what the animal looks like, where it lives and something of the feeling of the surrounding countryside?

This can only be achieved by carefully choosing the right setting for the picture. A few years ago I wrote a book on the wildlife of Snowdonia National Park; it was a project close to my heart. As a baby my first ever holidays were taken in these mountains and I have returned to them countless times since. I really wanted the photographs to pass on my feelings for the landscape.

Wild animals are inextricably linked to their habitat. They cannot survive without an environment to support, feed and shelter them. Equally, animals help to mould and shape their surroundings simply by leading their normal lives.

For me, the best wildlife photographs show animals in their surroundings. They reveal what the subject looks like and exactly where it lives. Snowdonia is a complex place but the essence of the mountains can be summed up in three words – water, rocks and wildlife. This picture has all three. After twenty-five years of photography in Snowdonia, this is my favourite picture.

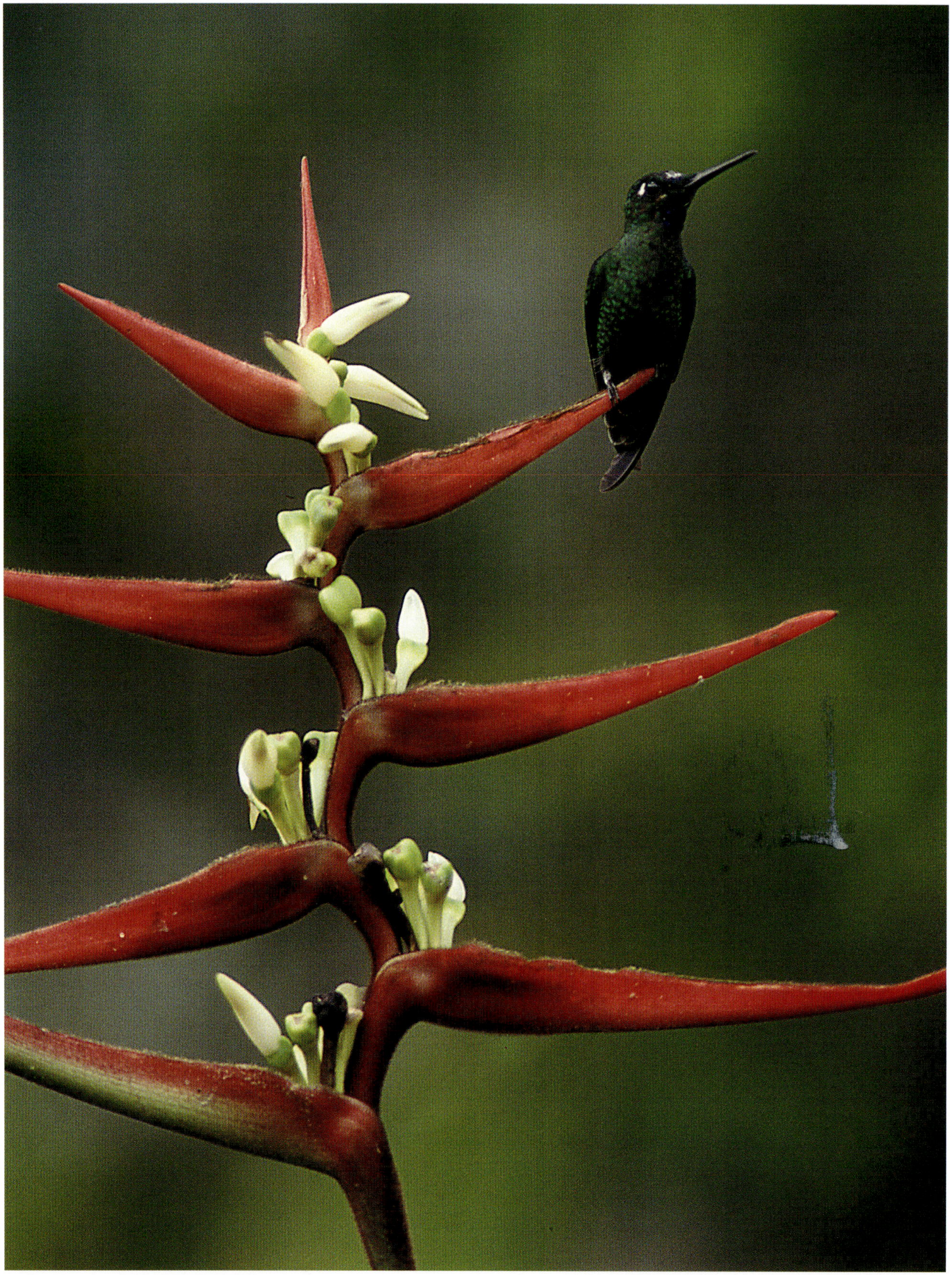

In the stunningly beautiful cloud forests of the Andes Mountains in South America, there lives a hummingbird no longer than my index finger. The Andean Emerald is not a particularly shy creature, it will feed while surrounded by humans. Getting close is not a problem; the real difficulty lies in the fact that these birds never stop moving.

The combination of a very fast metabolic rate and a high-energy diet allows the tiny hummingbird to constantly zip around the forest like a hyperactive shadow. Pausing only to investigate open flowers, the Andean Emerald searches endlessly for the nectar that makes up its specialised food supply. Photography is extremely frustrating: the bird has usually vanished before a single picture can be taken.

The Andean Emerald does occasionally rest but only for a couple of seconds. When it decides to sit on a branch of heliconia, the opportunity is too good to miss. The camera was aimed, focused and fired in less than a second. This is definitely not a recommended technique but it's often the only option. The tropical flower was a perfect backdrop for the delicate hummingbird and the captivating scene was recorded on film before the exquisite creature darted off to resume its endless search.

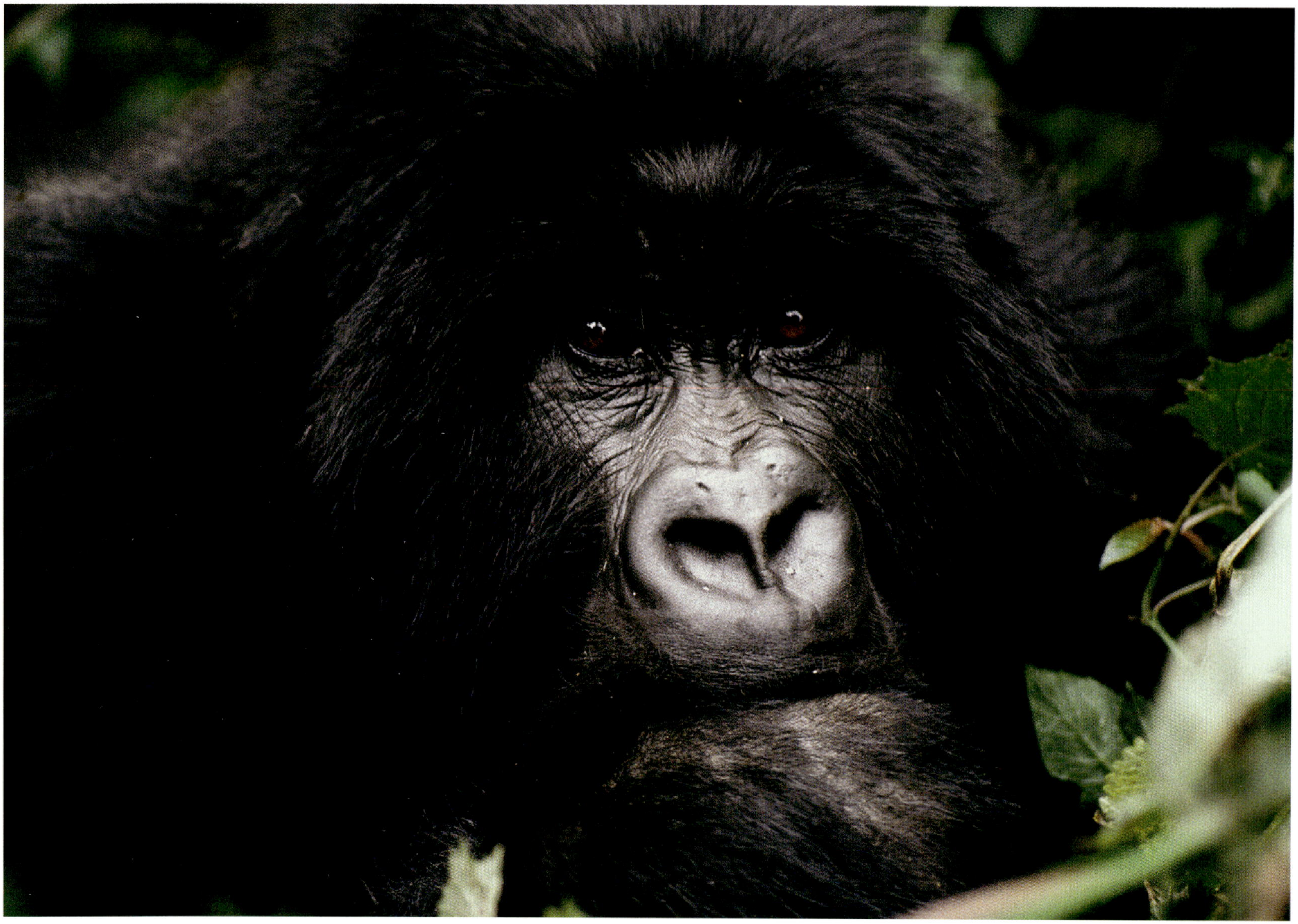

Of all the wildlife I have ever encountered, anywhere in the world, there has been one species more than any other that has completely captured my imagination. Mountain gorillas.

In popular mythology gorillas are portrayed as bloodthirsty killers that will attack humans on sight. Nothing could be further from the truth. Gorillas are gentle, peaceful vegetarians that are just as frightened of us as we are of them. The gorillas' response to the presence of a man is not to fight, but to run away. It takes a while to persuade these naturally shy animals to accept close contact with humans. But the effort is repaid a thousand-fold. Once the gorillas realise that they are not going to be attacked, they begin to behave normally and, sometimes, interest can then become mutual.

On my second day with a group close to the border with Zaire, I sat with a fully-grown gorilla in the rainforests of the Virunga Mountains. We were within touching distance but just looked at each other. Intelligence and curiosity radiated from the gorilla's warm, friendly, hazel brown eyes and I was captivated. After a while the gorilla stood and slowly walked off on all fours, resting her considerable weight on callused knuckles. There was no uncomfortable aftertaste of threat or intimidation, the gorilla had displayed a healthy interest in another, slightly unusual, animal. Which is exactly what I was doing.

Today there are only around 600 mountain gorillas left alive.

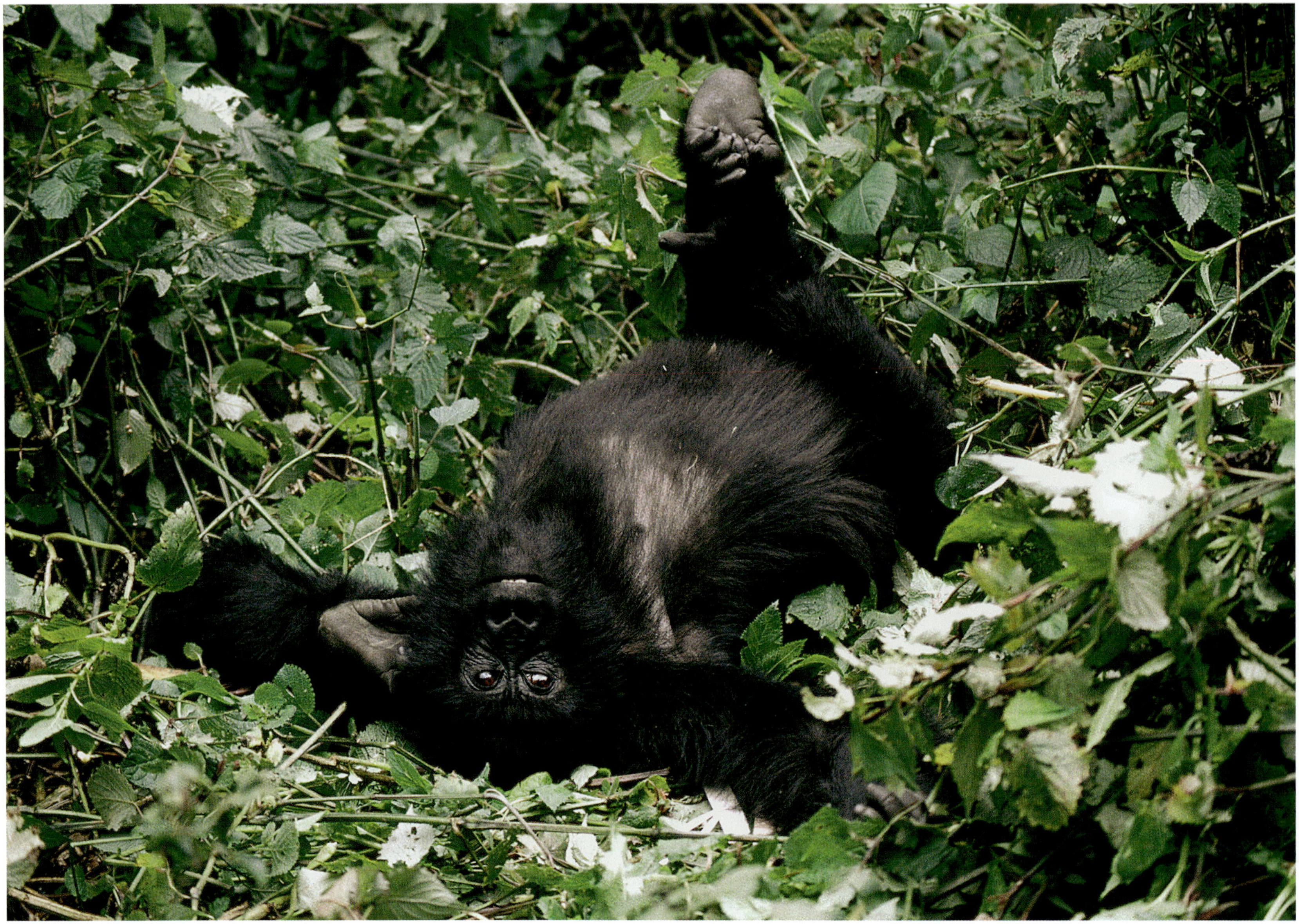

Adult gorillas are occasionally playful but, as with humans, it is the youngsters that are real experts at amusing themselves. To get the most unexpected photographs I quickly learned to follow eager adolescents as they explored the forest. Between the age of three and six years old the gorillas are confident enough to be independent but not yet old enough to take on the more serious role of being an adult.

To a young gorilla everything is a potential toy. Leaves, branches, stones and human visitors are all objects of intense interest. Occasionally an excited four year old would rush past and touch me with one hand, before suddenly noticing the wonderful bouncing effect produced by tugging at an overhead branch. When the branch was finally ripped from the tree, it was time to gnaw the shoulders of a sibling or investigate the properties of a large flat stone. The forest is full of fascination to a growing gorilla.

This youngster had just tried to explore my camera bag and was thwarted by the complexities of the zip fastenings. Having lost interest in his inaccessible booty, the exuberant gorilla performed a serious of elegant somersaults and lay on his back playing with his toes. Maybe some people could watch this child-like behaviour and not find that their heart has melted, but I'm not one of them.

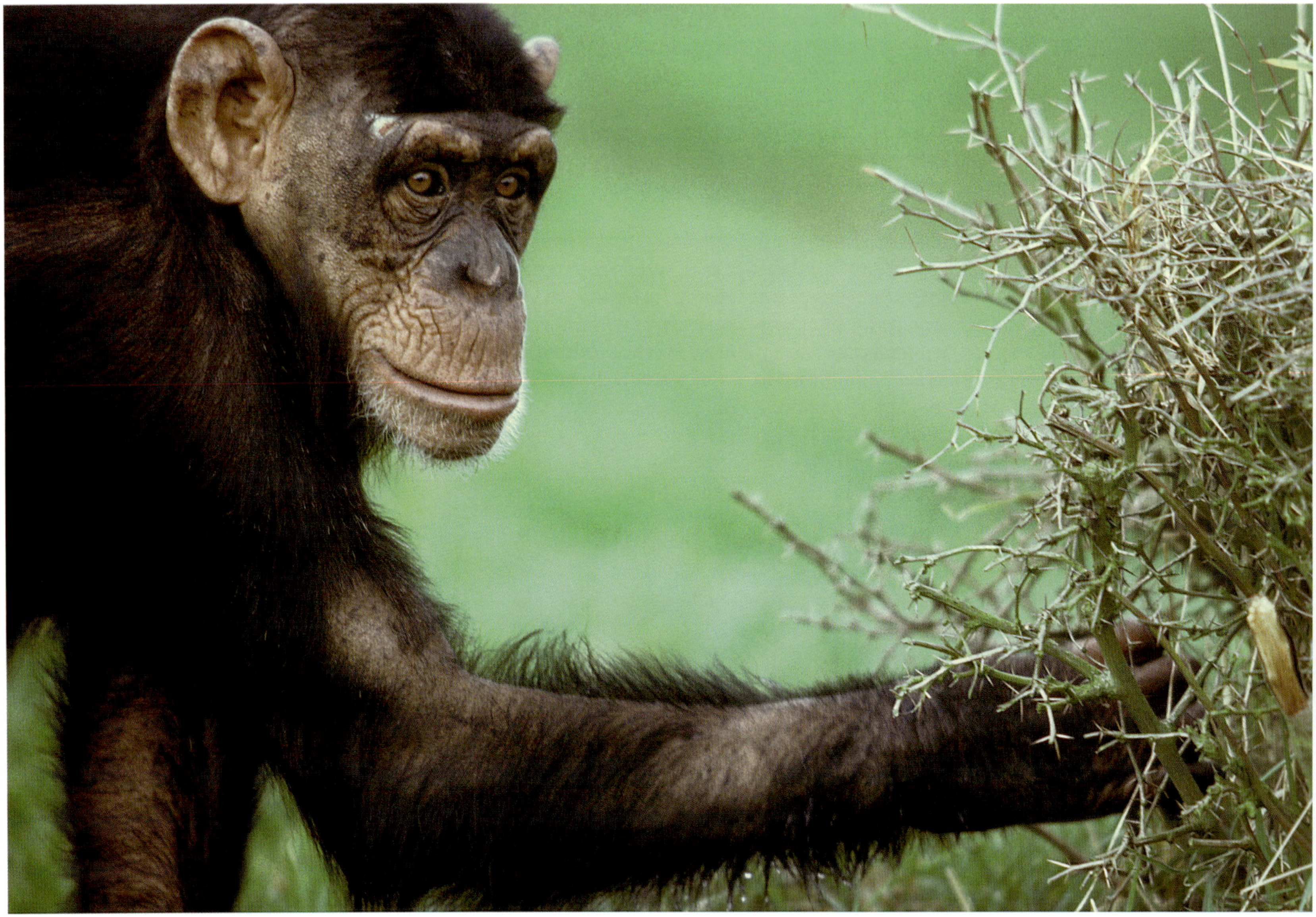

Chimpanzees are just as interesting as gorillas but in very different ways. The two species are closely related but have their own distinct personalities. While gorillas are usually quiet and reserved, chimps are restless and argumentative. Chimpanzee aggression can flare up and dissolve in a matter of minutes; they can shift from bouts of bloodcurdling anger to whimsical playfulness in the blink of an eye.

Of course this quixotic behaviour makes them perfect subjects for a camera. Their physical appearance alone is enough to grab our attention; chimpanzees are just too human-like for us to ignore. For this reason many people are not totally comfortable with chimps. Scientists call this response the 'ape syndrome'; it's defined as a feeling of discomfort when faced with animals that are members of our own family. For me this is a major part of the fascination.

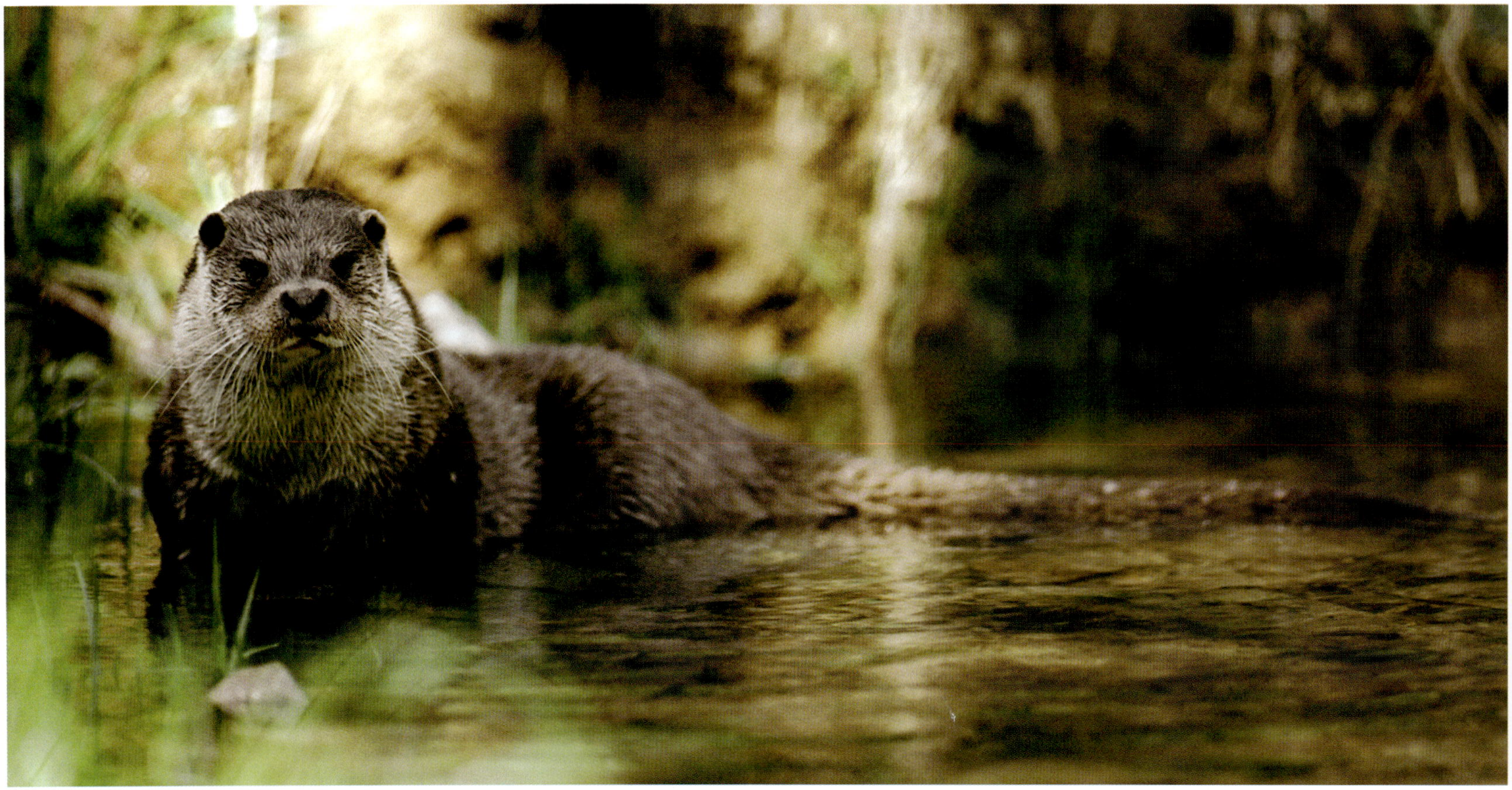

Some animals possess an intangible star quality that is impossible to define, yet stands out even to the most unobservant. Otters have this presence in abundance. They are one of the world's most photogenic animals. Otters never seem to do anything that wouldn't look good on film.

For a few decades in the middle of the twentieth century the otter population suffered terribly. Their numbers dropped to dangerously low levels. But a series of conservation projects have completely reversed this trend. Pollution control has cleaned up the rivers and allowed fish numbers to increase, hunting was banned and captive-bred otters have been selectively released into the wild. Otters are once again fishing in many of our waterways, and it's wonderful to see them again.

In addition to their aesthetic qualities, otters are important to me because they were the species that launched my career. My first real commission was to illustrate a book on otters of the world. I have never stopped being grateful to them.

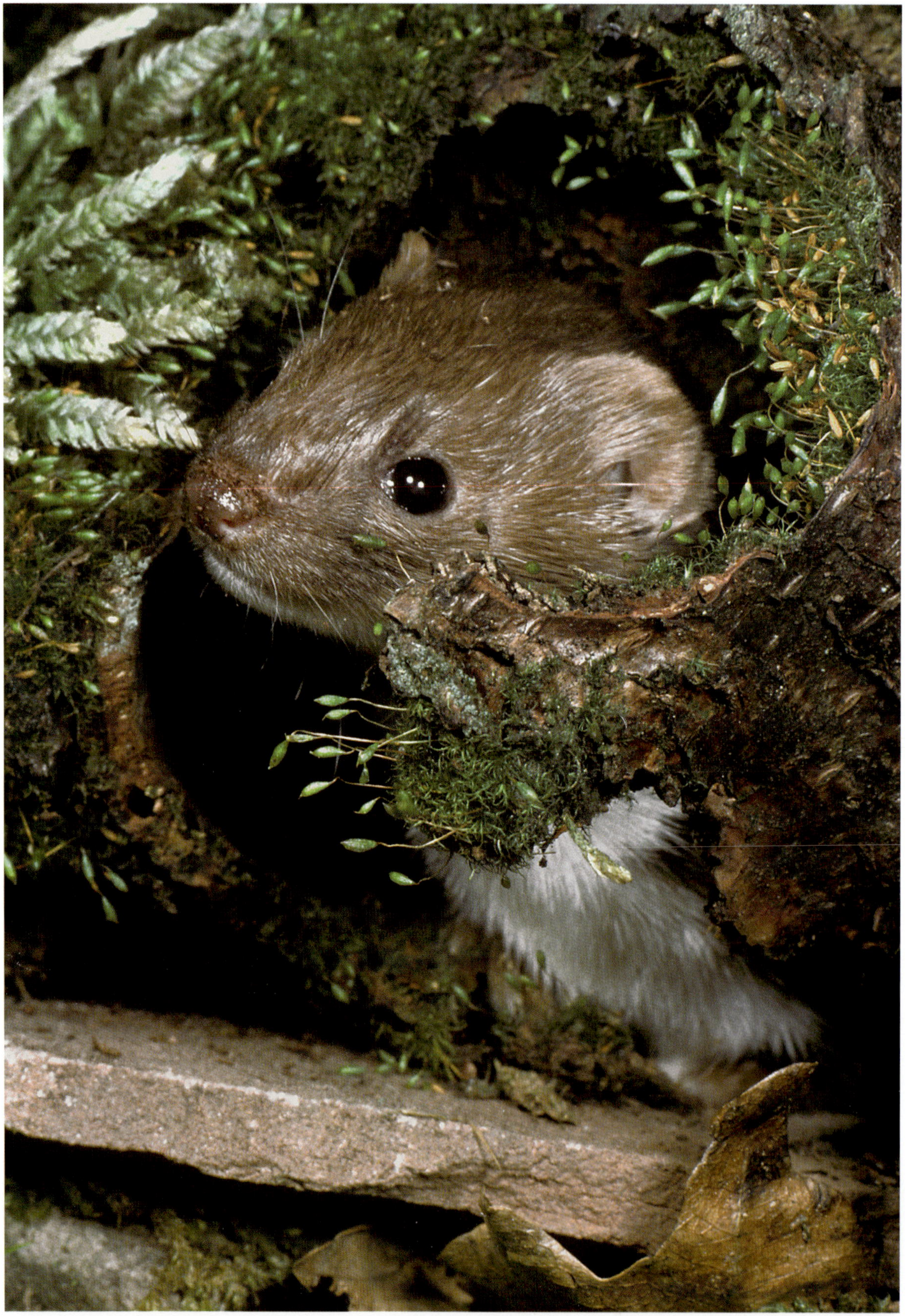

Otters are members of a family known as the mustelids. These are a group of long-bodied, short-legged hunters that are, usually, shy and retiring. The weasel is the smallest British member of the mustelids. No longer than a pencil, these tiny hunters can be found almost everywhere, apart from the most densely built-up areas. Weasels are furtive shadows that inhabit woodlands, hedgerows and undergrowth; they have a reasonably healthy population – yet most people have never seen one.

The truth is that weasels are only ever seen when crossing roads, and these are frustrating encounters. When a slender, low-slung silhouette darts across the tarmac, it will have disappeared before anyone has time to take a closer look. The distinctive shape and movement are the only clues to the owner's identity. Fast and sinuous, weasels move with an impossible grace that reminds me of water trickling down a tortuous mountain stream. Weasels don't run – they flow.

But, despite their size, weasels are awesome hunters. If weasels were the size of dogs, they would be the most fiercesome predators on Earth. They can take prey far heavier than themselves, including young rabbits. Weasels often search for food by exploring underground tunnels and investigating holes in dry stone walls. They use an acute sense of smell to track down the small mammals that make their home in these safe crevices. It is here that their slim, lithe physique is at its most useful. Weasels can twist and turn through the narrowest passages, even bending their bodies into right angles when pushing through tunnels.

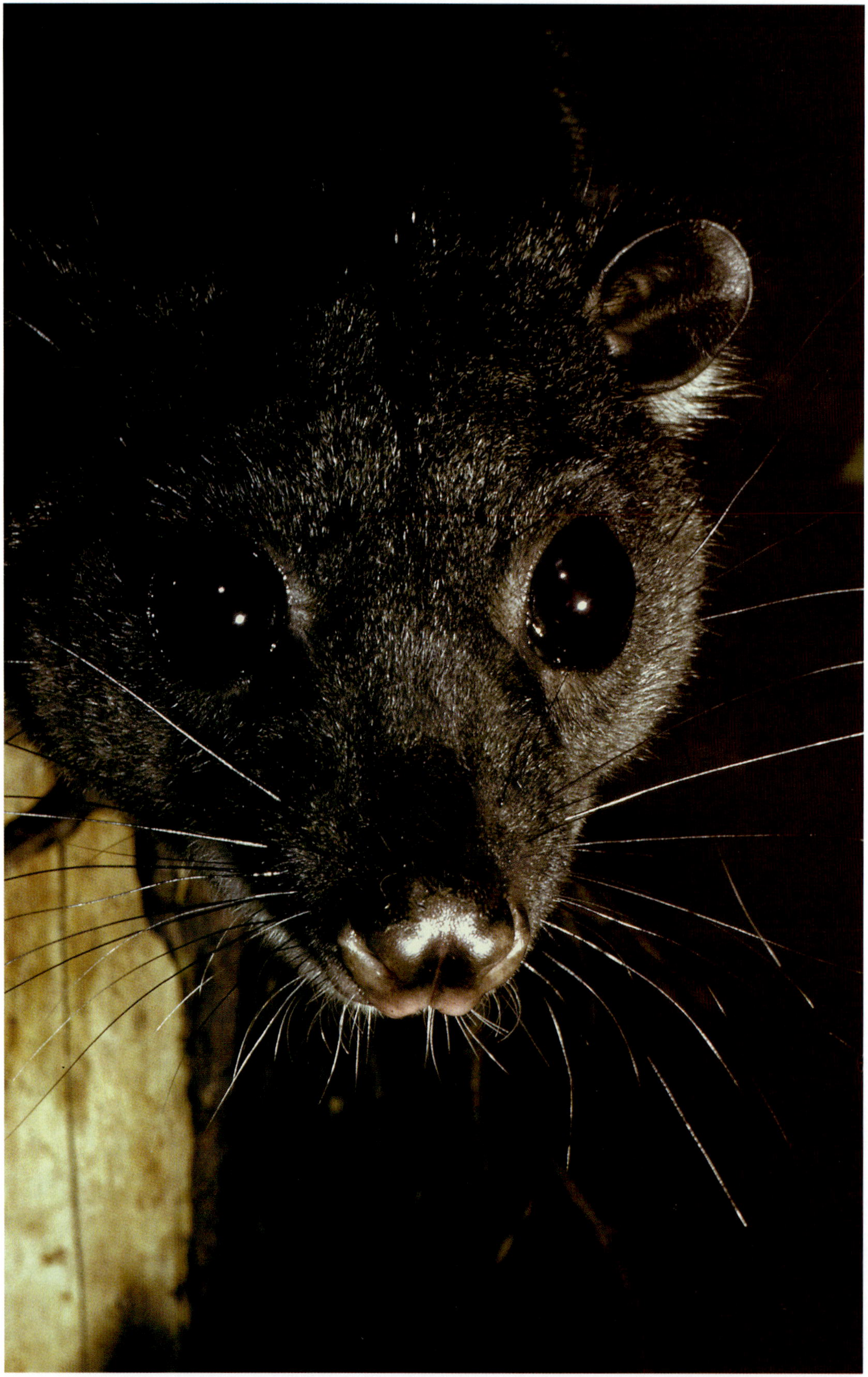

The ground cuscus is an elusive nocturnal opossum, a marsupial that is related to koalas and kangaroos. One of ten known species of cuscus, this particular animal is an omnivore that lives in the forests of New Guinea. It is equally at home in the treetops and on the forest floor.

A century ago the French Impressionist Claude Monet said ‘light is the principal person in the picture’. Of course he was talking about painting but, with just a little biological reapplication, the idea applies equally well to wildlife photography.

I enjoy this portrait because it was an experiment with light. This photograph is one of those that worked.

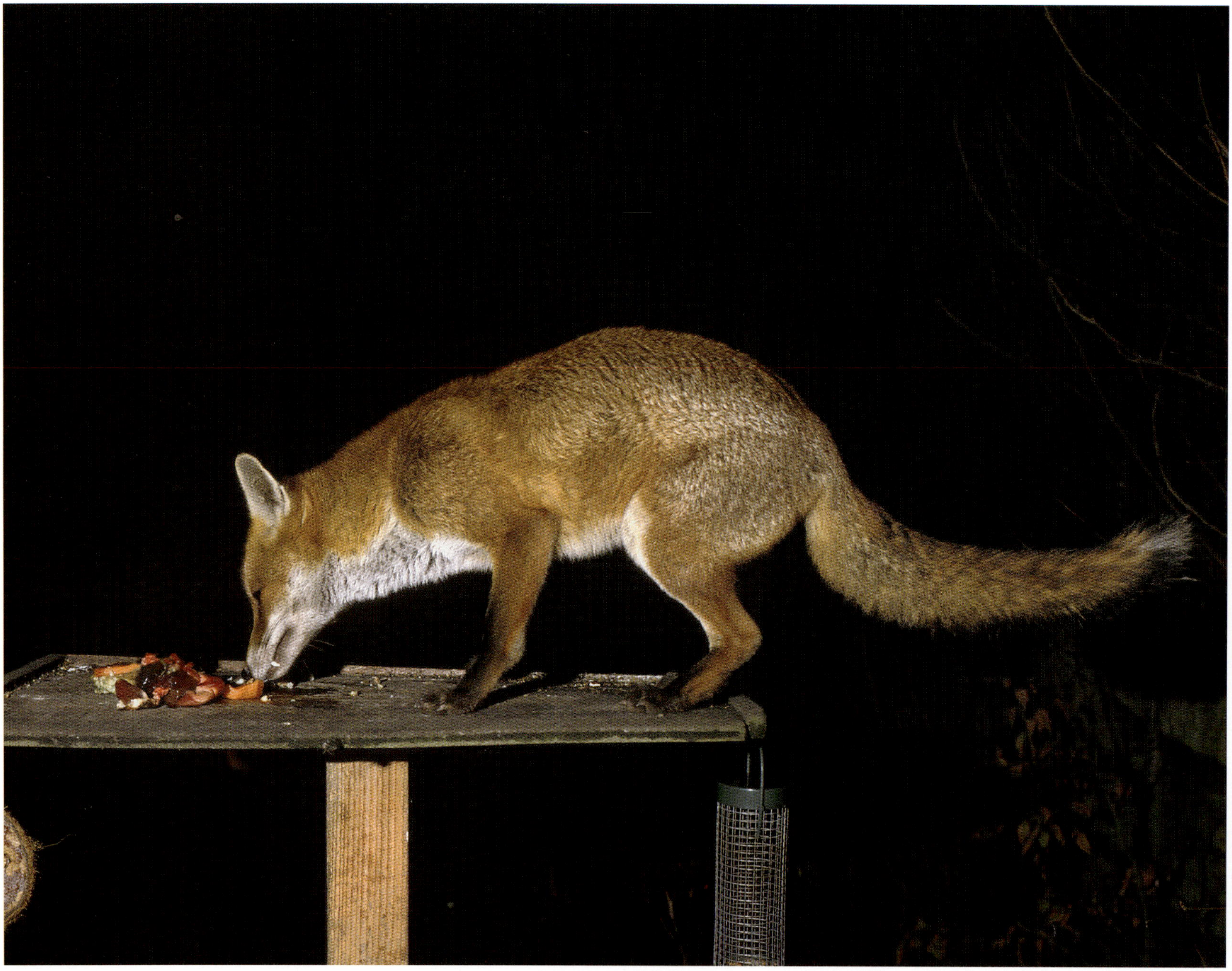

No matter how many people take wildlife photographs, there will never come a point when everything has been accomplished. There is a finite number of animals and an apparently infinite number of people trying to capture them on film. So, logically, it would seem that eventually there would be nothing new to photograph.

But the natural world constantly moves on as the landscape alters and evolves. And human activity inevitably accelerates this transformation. The countryside we see now is very different to that of just 100 years ago; photographs taken today would have been impossible in any earlier age.

Many people in the west are sufficiently affluent to be selective about their food; we eat what we like and throw away the rest. We are also concerned about the welfare of our local wildlife and the two factors come together in the form of bird tables. These would have been an outrageous concept in the nineteenth century, when nothing was wasted and wild animals were simply an irrelevance. But now every corner of the country has its own motley collection of expensive designer-built tables or rough-hewn platforms specifically created to keep birds alive.

But birds are not the only animals that benefit from our generosity. Quick-witted foxes have learned to investigate any bird-tables within their hunting territory. Unless they are particularly hungry, foxes ignore the scent of bread or peanuts. But meat is a different matter. Foxes are agile and quite capable of scrambling along a fence or leaping onto a low table – if the reward is sufficiently tasty. This is relatively new behaviour and, so far, has only been seen in foxes that live in areas where householders are particularly charitable and the pickings are rich.

As long as our surroundings keep changing, and wild animals learn to adapt, there will always be something new to see and photograph.

Index

For those with the technology, more information on Michael Leach's work can be seen at *www.michael-leach.co.uk*